Artificial Lures

MINNETONKA, MINNESOTA

Author Dick Sternberg is a versatile multi-species angler, using artificial lures to catch everything from sunfish to salmon.

Artificial Lures

Tom Carpenter
Creative Director

Michele Teigen
Senior Book Development Coordinator

**Bill Lindner Photography (Bill Lindner, Tom Heck, Mike Hehner and Pete Cozad),
Phil Aarrestad, Christopher M. Batin,
Dick Sternberg**
Photography

Dave Schelitzche
Illustration

Julie Cisler, Dave Schelitzche
Book Design & Production

Gina Germ
Photo Editor

6 7 8 9 / 05 04 03 02

ISBN 1-581590-06-7

North American Fishing Club
12301 Whitewater Drive
Minnetonka, MN 55343
www.fishingclub.com

CONTENTS

INTRODUCTION

In their most basic form, artificial lures are nothing more than hunks of wood or bits of plastic and metal crafted to look like something a fish would want to eat.

So why are they so intriguing?

Artificial Lures, written by former fisheries biologist and angling expert Dick Sternberg, explores the major classes of artificial lures available to today's anglers. It highlights the situations where each class or bait performs best.

Expert anglers will appreciate the dozens of tips for making their artificial lures more effective, while beginners will learn where, when and how to use them.

Artificial Lures also helps you select the proper tackle for the baits you use. After all, the right rod can mean the difference between success and failure, as can something as simple as the knot you choose.

Enjoy *Artificial Lures*, your personal guide to the many baits gracing your tacklebox.

Steve Pennaz
Executive Director
North American
Fishing Club

SUBSURFACE PLUGS

*S*ubsurface plugs are among the oldest of gamefish lures, and they are just as effective now as ever.

SUBSURFACE PLUGS

Webster's Dictionary defines a plug as "an artificial angling lure used primarily for casting and made with one or more sets of gang hooks." Some plugs are designed for surface fishing; others, to run beneath the surface. This chapter deals with the latter.

To be a little more specific, subsurface plugs usually have a wooden or plastic body shaped like a baitfish. But a few models are designed to mimic crayfish, waterdogs or other aquatic fare.

Following are the most popular types of subsurface plugs:
- **Crankbaits** - A crankbait has a plastic or metal lip at the front that gives the lure a side-to-side wiggling or wobbling action and causes it to dive.
- **Minnowbaits** - Similar to a crankbait, a minnowbait also has a front lip, but the body is slimmer for its length.
- **Vibrating Plugs** -These plugs have a thin body with the attachment eye on the back, giving them a tight wiggling action.
- **Trolling Plugs** - These plugs vary greatly in shape, but most have a broad, flat forehead which makes them quite wind-resistant and difficult to cast. Normally fished by trolling, they have an intense wobble.
- **Jerkbaits** - Used primarily for large pike and muskies, these giant plugs have no built-in action. They dart erratically from side to side when retrieved with downward sweeps of the rod.
- **Magnum Bass Plugs** - These huge plugs, usually made of wood, have an extremely wide wobble. Although they were originally designed for giant Florida bass, anglers have found them to be effective for many other kinds of large gamefish.

Plug-Selection Guide

Fish Species	Plug Length
Crappie	1-2 inches
Small trout	1-3 inches
White bass	$1^1/_2$-3 inches
Smallmouth and spotted bass	2-3 inches
Northern largemouth bass	2-6 inches
Walleye	3-6 inches
Large trout and salmon	3-7 inches
Northern pike, muskie, striper and Florida largemouth bass	4-12 inches

Jerkbait

Magnum bass plug

Vibrating plug

Trolling plug

Minnowbait

Crankbait

CRANKBAITS

The tempting wobble of a crankbait often triggers fish to bite, even when they're not actively feeding. Although crankbaits work best at water temperatures above 55°F, they can be retrieved very slowly to catch fish at much lower temperatures.

Crankbaits are most often used for casting, but they can also be trolled. Because crankbaits are usually retrieved at a relatively fast speed, they're ideal for covering a lot of water in a hurry.

Any kind of gamefish that feeds on baitfish can be caught on a crankbait. Anglers use crankbaits only an inch or two long for species such as crappies, white bass and trout, while 8- to 12-inchers are commonly used for pike, muskies, stripers and big largemouth.

Crankbaits are effective in water of most any clarity. Even in very muddy water, fish can detect a crankbait's wobble using their lateral-line system. Most anglers agree that a crankbait with a tight wiggle works better in low-clarity water than one with a loose wobble. Internal rattles also make it easier for fish to locate the bait.

Because crankbaits have exposed hooks, they are not the best choice for fishing in dense weeds or other heavy cover. But they are not as prone to snagging or fouling as many anglers believe. The lip runs interference for the hooks, deflecting off rocks and logs. And, in some types of weeds, a rapid retrieve will shatter the leaves, so they don't foul the hooks.

You can also minimize snagging or fouling by selecting a crankbait that runs at the proper depth. If the weeds top out at 10 feet, for instance, choose a crankbait that runs at that depth. This way, the bait will occasionally tick the weedtops, but won't dive way into the weeds. A crankbait with a straight lip is less prone to snagging because it runs nose-down, minimizing the chances that the hooks will contact the cover.

In selecting a crankbait, the most important considerations are running depth and action. The way a crankbait performs depends on the following:

• **Lip Design** - The running depth of a crankbait depends primarily on the size, shape and angle of the lip. In general, the larger the lip and the straighter its angle in relation to the plug's

Shallow Runners

Medium Runners

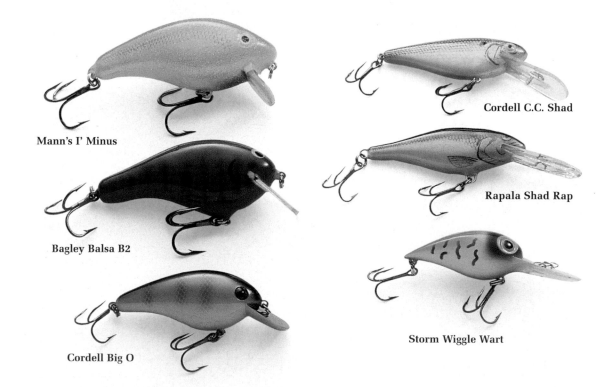

Mann's I' Minus

Bagley Balsa B2

Cordell Big O

Cordell C.C. Shad

Rapala Shad Rap

Storm Wiggle Wart

Shallow runners track at depths of 1 to 7 feet; medium runners, 8 to 15 feet and deep runners, more than 15 feet. Running depth depends mainly on the size and angle of the lip (opposite).

How the Lip Affects Running Depth

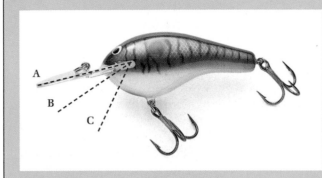

A deep-running crankbait has a lip at an angle of no more than (a) 10 degrees to the plug's horizontal axis; a medium-running crankbait, no more than (b) 30 degrees and a shallow-running crankbait, no less than (c) 60 degrees.

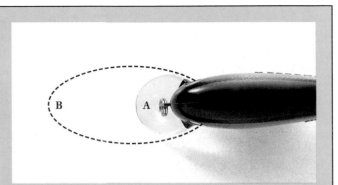

A shallow-running crankbait normally has (a) a shorter, narrower lip than (b) a deep-runner. The lip of a medium runner is intermediate in shape.

horizontal axis, the deeper the plug will dive.

The shape and angle of the lip also affects a crankbait's action. The wider the lip, the more side-to-side wobble. The greater the angle of the lip, the more roll.

Deep Runners

Mann's 20+

Rapala Down Deep Rattlin' Fat Rap

Storm Lightnin' Shad

The position of the plug's attachment eye also affects its action. A plug with an eye close to the nose or on the nose will roll more than one with the eye farther down the lip.

• **Body Material** - The majority of crankbaits have hollow plastic, foamed plastic or wooden bodies, so they float at rest. Hard-plastic crankbaits are the most durable and the best choice for casting. But foamed plastic or wooden ones are lighter and more responsive, so they have more action on a slow retrieve. Balsa crankbaits, though relatively expensive, are the lightest and most responsive of all.

Although most crankbaits float, some have internal lead

weights to make them sink or suspend. A bait that sinks can be counted down to reach fish at any depth; one that suspends can be fished very slowly, yet will not float up like a normal crankbait.

• **Body Shape** - The shape of a crankbait's body affects its action and stability. As a rule, the thinner the body, the tighter and faster the wobble. But a thin-bodied bait does not run as true as one with a fatter body; it is more likely to tip to the side and lose depth as you increase the retrieve speed. It is also harder to keep a thin-bodied bait in tune (p. 11).

Roll (left) vs. wobble (right)

How to Fish Crankbaits

Crankin' has emerged as one of the top tournament fishing methods, and for good reason. No other technique enables you to cover so much water in such a short period of time.

An angler who is not familiar with a body of water can use crankbaits to search out prime fishing areas. When he starts catching fish, he may then switch over to a slower method that allows him to strain the water more thoroughly.

Fishermen also use crankbaits to fish a "milk run" consisting of several key pieces of structure or cover. They make a few casts in one spot, hoping to tempt the active feeders, and then quickly move on to the next. This technique is usually more effective than camping on a good spot, waiting for the fish to turn on.

The main consideration in crankbait fishing is selecting a lure that runs at the right depth. If you're fishing a rock pile that tops off at 15 feet, for instance, you want a crankbait capable of reaching that depth or even a little deeper. That means you may snag up once in a while, but that's better than selecting a lure than runs only 12 feet deep and never gets snagged.

You can determine a crankbait's running depth by referring to a depth chart (opposite), but the surest method is testing it yourself. Experiment by making casts in different water depths until you determine the depth at which the lure just "ticks" bottom.

A crankbait's running depth varies somewhat depending on line diameter, line length and retrieve speed.

The thinner your line, the deeper the lure will run, because there is less water resistance against your line. Some crankbait anglers are switching to superlines, because they have a thinner diameter for their strength.

Crankbait trollers know that they can reach greater depths by letting out more line – up to a point. After that, it makes no difference how much line you let out, the lure will only run so deep. This explains why long casts are so important in crankbait fishing. You must cast well past your target so the lure has time to reach its maximum running depth before it gets to the fish zone.

Many anglers share the mistaken belief that the faster they retrieve, the deeper their crankbait will run. But, in fact, every crankbait has an optimum retrieve speed. If you retrieve slower or faster, the lure will not run as deep. The only way to determine the perfect speed is to experiment.

For a crankbait to reach its maximum depth, it must be properly tuned, meaning that it tracks perfectly straight. If the attachment eye is bent even the slightest bit to one side or the other, the lure will veer to the side and lose depth. You can tune your crankbait by bending the eye as shown on the opposite page.

Veteran crankbait anglers know that an erratic retrieve triggers more strikes than a steady one. They make every effort to retrieve the lure so it periodically bumps the bottom or some type of cover, interrupting its action. When fishing in woody cover, for instance, they intentionally aim their casts so the bait will bump a stump or log as they reel in.

If there is no cover to alter the lure's action, try a stop-and-go retrieve. Reel rapidly, pause for a second and let the bait float up slightly, then reel rapidly again. Strikes often come on the pause.

How fast you retrieve depends not only on the particular lure you're using, but also on water temperature. As a rule, the cooler the water, the slower your retrieve. But you may also want to slow down your retrieve when fish are in a negative mood.

When fish strike a fast-moving crankbait, they normally hook themselves. But if a fish grabs the lure from behind, you may just feel the line go slack or notice a slight change in its action. Whenever you feel anything out of the ordinary, set the hook.

Recommended Tackle

For heavy cover, where lines up to 25-pound test are required, most anglers opt for baitcasting gear. Because lengthy casts are important in crankbait fishing, it pays to use a long rod, $6\frac{1}{2}$ to $7\frac{1}{2}$ feet, for extra casting leverage. Many anglers prefer a rod with a soft tip, which allows the fish to take the bait farther into its mouth before you set the hook. The reel should have a high gear ratio, at least 5:1, which enables a rapid retrieve.

A spinning outfit with 6- to 12-pound mono is adequate for fishing crankbaits in open water or light cover.

Tips for Fishing Crankbaits

Refer to a depth chart to determine how deep a certain crankbait will run with various amounts of line. Such charts require a correction factor for use with different line diameters.

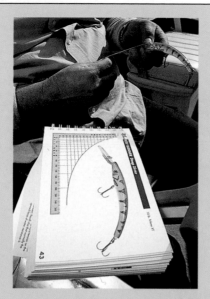

Bump your crankbait off of rocks, logs or other obstructions; the sudden change of action often triggers a strike.

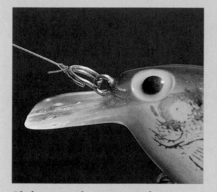

If the attachment eye has a split ring, tie your line directly to it. Extra hardware adds weight and inhibits the lure's action.

If the lure has a plain wire eye, attach your line with a round-nosed snap. Don't use a sharp-nosed snap or a bulky snap-swivel.

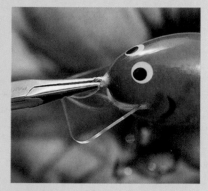

Tune a crankbait by bending the attachment eye in the direction opposite to that in which the lure is tracking. If it's tracking to the left, for example, bend the eye to the right and then test the action.

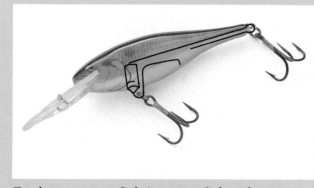

For large, strong-fighting gamefish, select a crankbait with hooks attached to an internal wire. Screw eyes may pull out.

Clip off the leading points on a crankbait's treble hooks when fishing in weedy cover. The remaining points are turned up and much less likely to foul in the vegetation.

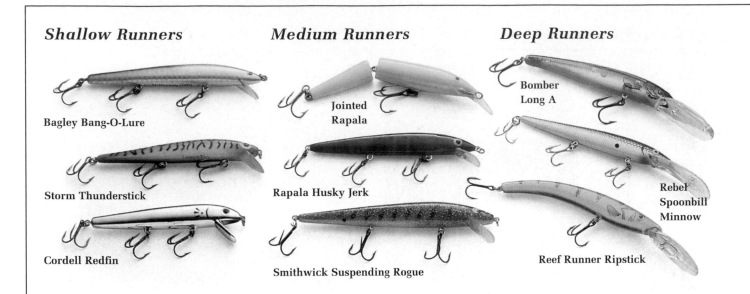

Shallow Runners

Bagley Bang-O-Lure

Storm Thunderstick

Cordell Redfin

Medium Runners

Jointed Rapala

Rapala Husky Jerk

Smithwick Suspending Rogue

Deep Runners

Bomber Long A

Rebel Spoonbill Minnow

Reef Runner Ripstick

MINNOWBAITS

Minnowbaits bear many similarities to crankbaits, but there are some significant differences:

• The body of a minnowbait is longer and slimmer, so it more closely resembles the shape of slim-bodied baitfish, such as shiners.

• The lip is smaller and usually narrower, so the lure has a tight rocking action rather than a wide, side-to-side wobble. This type of action more closely resembles that of a swimming baitfish, but produces much less vibration.

• Because of its smaller lip, a minnowbait generally runs shallower than a crankbait.

• The slimmer body of a minnowbait has less stability, meaning that slower retrieve speeds are normally required.

• Minnowbaits are comparatively light, so they're more difficult to cast than crankbaits.

Like crankbaits, minnowbaits come in shallow-, medium- and deep-running models, although the maximum depths for each of these categories is considerably shallower.

Extra-Deep Runners

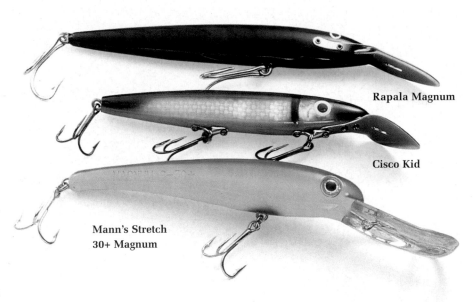

Rapala Magnum

Cisco Kid

Mann's Stretch 30+ Magnum

The first minnowbaits were made of balsa wood, and many still are. But plastic baits are gaining in popularity. Plastic baits are more durable and slightly heavier, so they are somewhat easier to cast. But balsa baits are more responsive and have more action at a slow retrieve speed.

Some "big-game" minnowbaits have thick plastic bodies and metal lips. They can be retrieved faster than ordinary minnowbaits and will stand up to toothy freshwater and saltwater gamefish.

Most minnowbaits float at rest, but some are weighted to sink. Sinking models can be counted down to the desired depth, but they have less rocking action than floaters.

Neutrally-buoyant minnowbaits are rapidly gaining popularity, because you can stop them during the retrieve without them floating up. Negative gamefish that refuse

moving baits may strike these baits on the pause.

The effectiveness of minnowbaits is due, in part, to their realistic look and action. But there's another even more important reason: most predator fish, given a choice, prefer slim-bodied baitfish to those with deep bodies. Slim-bodied forage is easier to swallow and less likely to wedge in the fish's throat.

This explains why many anglers prefer minnowbaits to crankbaits in clear water, where the fish can get a good look at the bait. Minnowbaits are not as effective as crankbaits in discolored water, however, because they produce considerably less vibration.

Minnowbaits are an excellent choice in cool water, because they can be retrieved more slowly and still retain

their action. But they do not work as well in weedy or snaggy cover; the smaller lip provides less protection for the hooks.

Shallow-running minnowbaits are one of the top lures for night fishing. They have enough buoyancy to be fished over shallow shoals or weedbeds without fouling, and fish can easily make out the plug's silhouette against the surface.

How to Fish Minnowbaits

Today, floating minnowbaits enjoy tremendous popularity, due mainly to their ultra-realistic action. No other bait so closely mimics a swimming minnow.

But floating minnowbaits can be difficult to cast, particularly when you're bucking the wind. That explains why most anglers use light spinning tackle and try to keep the wind at their back.

Floating minnowbaits are usually fished with a steady, slow- to moderate-speed retrieve. Or you can alternately speed them up and slow them down. But their high buoyancy makes them difficult to fish with a true stop-and-go retrieve, because they float up too far and too fast on the pause.

Another popular method for using a floating minnowbait is long-line trolling in shallow water. Simply let out a lot of line (as much as 200 feet), and pull the lure directly behind the boat. Because of the great distance between the boat and the lure, spooking is not much of a problem. If your lure is not running deep enough, add a split shot or two several feet up the line.

When bass are in the shallows, you can use a floating minnowbait as a topwater. Retrieve it with a twitch-and-pause motion, making it dive a few inches and then hesitating while it floats back to the surface.

For years, savvy fishermen recognized the need for a minnowbait that didn't float up on the pause, so they added lead weights to floating minnowbaits to make them neutrally buoyant. The small cadre of anglers who were familiar with this "secret

method" made astounding catches of bass, walleye and other gamefish, even under the worst fishing conditions.

But as the secret began to leak out, pre-weighted minnowbaits began to appear on the market. These baits, sometimes referred to as "jerkbaits," should not be confused with the large (sometimes giant) jerkbaits used for pike and muskie (p. 23).

Jerkbaits, as their name suggests, are fished with a jerky, stop-and-go retrieve. But when you stop, the bait hangs in the face of a following gamefish rather than floating up, greatly boosting the odds that the fish will strike.

Sinking minnowbaits are weighted even more heavily than jerkbaits, so they are easy to cast. To fish the lure near the bottom, allow it to sink until the line goes slack, reel it a short distance, and then allow it to sink again. To reach suspended fish, try counting it down to different depths before starting your retrieve. When you get a strike or hook a fish, repeat the same count on the next cast.

Although you can reach fish in deep water with sinking minnowbaits or deep-diving floaters, many experienced anglers prefer to use shallow-

running floaters fished with a variety of deep-trolling gear, such as downriggers, Snap-Weights (opposite), lead-core line or three-way rigs. Not only does this gear make it easier to control your depth, shallow-running floaters have an action superior to that of sinkers or deep-divers.

Sinking minnowbaits, because they are heavily weighted, do not have as much of the realistic rocking action of a typical narrow-lipped minnowbait. And deep-diving minnowbaits have an entirely different action; their long, broad lip gives them the wide wobble of a crankbait.

Recommended Tackle

For casting lightweight, shallow-running minnowbaits, use a medium-power spinning rod with a tip soft enough to flex from the lure's weight on the backcast. If your rod is too stiff, you'll have to throw the bait, because the tip won't do the work. Use a long-spool spinning reel filled nearly to the brim with 6- to 8-pound mono; go a little heavier when the fish are in cover.

You can also use spinning gear for casting weighted minnowbaits, but many anglers prefer medium- to medium-heavy-power baitcasting gear with 8- to 12-pound mono. The same baitcasting gear can also be used for trolling, but many fishermen prefer 10- to 20-pound-test superline because it has less water resistance and allows the lures to run deeper.

Tips for Fishing with Minnowbaits

Let out 100 to 150 feet of line, and then attach a Snap-Weight (inset). Continue letting out line until you feel the lure bump bottom, then reel up a few turns. When you hook a fish, reel down to the Snap-Weight and remove it before landing the fish.

Use a floating minnowbait as a surface lure by twitching it sharply, pausing to let it float back up and then twitching it again.

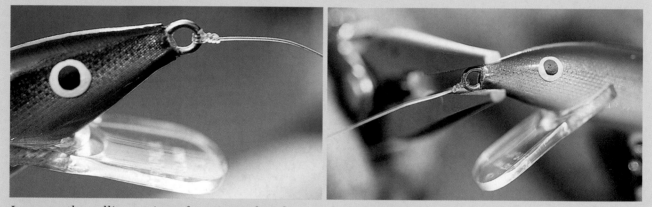

Increase the rolling action of a minnowbait by attaching it with a secure clinch knot, preferably one with a double line around the eye (left), and then pulling the knot slightly below the horizontal axis. Or, you can accomplish the same thing by bending the eye slightly downward (right).

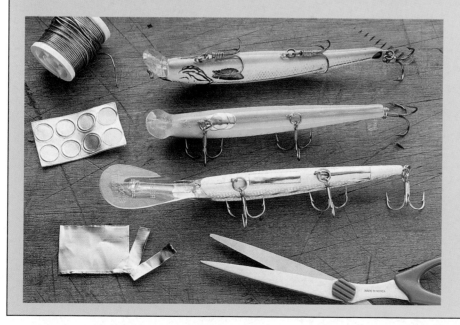

Add weight to a floating minnowbait to make it neutrally buoyant by wrapping the hooks with thin-diameter solder (top) or adding strips of golfer's tape to the lure's belly. The buoyancy of a pre-weighted jerkbait increases in cold water, but you can add enough weight to offset the additional flotation by adding small, adhesive-backed lead weights, such as Storm's SuspenDots (middle) or SuspenStrips (bottom).

VIBRATING PLUGS

Often called "lipless crankbaits," these thin-bodied plugs have a tighter wiggle than ordinary crankbaits and produce higher-frequency vibrations. Gamefish can easily detect these vibrations with their lateral-line systems, even in extremely murky water.

Like crankbaits, vibrating plugs appeal to practically any gamefish that feed on minnows or other baitfish. But because of their deep, thin body shape, they work especially well for species that feed on shad, sunfish or other deep-bodied forage. Vibrating plugs weighing as little as $\frac{1}{8}$ ounce are used for crappies and white bass, while models weighing up to $1\frac{1}{2}$ ounces are popular for striped bass, big largemouths and pike.

Because they do not have a lip to make them dive, the majority of vibrating plugs are designed to sink. Some have solid plastic bodies; others, hollow-plastic bodies filled with shot. The shot not only makes the lure sink, it produces a rattling sound.

Vibrating plugs are heavy for their size, so they cast easily. You can count them down to any depth (opposite), and you can even use them as a deep-water jigging bait, allowing them to sink to the bottom then jigging them vertically in the same manner as you would a jigging spoon (p. 104).

Because it has no lip to run interference for the hooks, a vibrating plug is more prone to snagging than a crankbait. But depth control is much easier, so you can avoid snagging or fouling by keeping the lure just above or along the edge of the cover.

For maximum wiggle, always attach a vibrating plug with a loop knot, split-ring or small, round-nosed snap, not a heavy snap-swivel.

Vibrating Plugs

Cordell Super Spot

Rapala Rattlin' Rap

Mann's Manniac

Bill Lewis Rat-L-Trap

The Countdown Technique

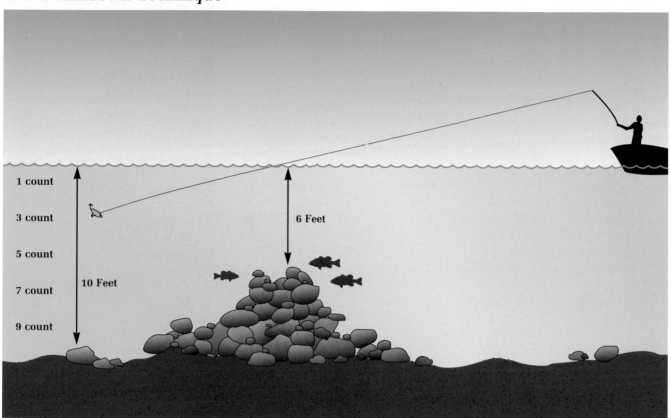

Make a long cast and then count the seconds as the lure sinks on a slack line; if it takes 5 seconds to reach bottom in 10 feet of water, the sink rate is 2 feet per second. You can then use this rate to calculate the depth of subsequent retrieves. To reach these fish on a 6-foot-deep rock pile, for example, let the plug sink for 3 seconds before starting to reel. Retrieve at a moderate speed to keep the lure at the desired depth as long as possible. Too fast, and the lure will run too shallow; too slow, and it will run too deep.

Bill Lewis Super Trap

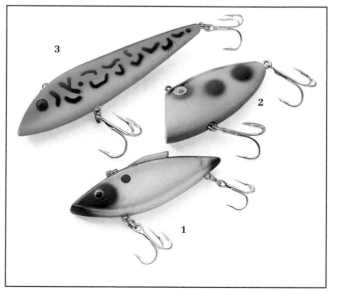

Vibrating plugs have the attachment eye on the back, creating an extremely tight wiggle rather than a loose wobble. Although most models have (1) a shad-shaped body, some have a (2) sharply sloping forehead or (3) a sleeker body.

TROLLING PLUGS

Although you can troll with most any kind of subsurface plug, trolling plugs are intended mainly for that purpose. Most of these lures have a broad forehead, a long snout or a flattened or scooped-out face that gives them a very wide wobble or an erratic action.

Most trolling plugs are made of hollow plastic, so they float. The majority of these lures run at depths of only 5 to 15 feet, but can be trolled much deeper by adding sinkers or using downriggers, diving planers, lead-core line (opposite) or three-way-swivel rigs.

While you can fish these lures by casting, they tend to be wind-resistant or prone to tangling. And many of them are too heavy to cast, unless you use heavy gear.

Trolling plugs work well for fishing expanses of open water or large flats. They're most often used for open-water species such as striped bass, trout and salmon, but they're also effective for walleyes, pike, muskies and bass when they're suspended or holding along a weedline.

For maximum water coverage, many trollers rely on side planers or trolling boards (pages 20-21). These devices move the lure away

Recommended Tackle

An ordinary medium-heavy power baitcasting outfit with 10- to 20-pound test superline works well for most plug-trolling situations.

For downrigger trolling, use a 7 1/2- to 8 1/2-foot, soft-tipped trolling rod and a high-capacity level-wind reel spooled with 12- to 20-pound test mono.

For lead-line trolling, select a heavy-power trolling rod and a high-capacity trolling reel spooled with 18- to 40-pound-test metered lead-core.

For speed-trolling, use a stiff trolling rod no more than 5 1/2 feet long. A lighter rod would bend too much from the strain of high-speed trolling.

Common Types of Trolling Plugs

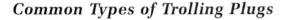

Broad-forehead style (Lazy Ike)

Long-snout style (Drifter Tackle The Believer)

Speed-trolling plug (Spoonplug)

Scooped-out-face style (Luhr Jensen J-Plug)

How to Troll with Lead-Core Line

Tie a barrel swivel to the end of the lead-core, and then attach a 6- to 10-foot, 12- to 20-pound-test mono leader with a round-nosed clip at the end for attaching the plug.

Let out line until you feel the lure bumping bottom, and then reel up a few turns so the lure bumps only occasionally. Let out more line when the water gets deeper; reel in when it gets shallower.

Most lead-core line changes color every 10 yards. When fishing for suspended fish, pay close attention to line color. Then, should you hook a fish, you can easily return to the same color.

Cover more water by placing long (8-foot-plus) trolling rods in horizontal rod holders placed at a right angle to the transom. Other rods can be fished directly out the back.

from the boat's wake, reducing the spooking factor.

Depending on their design, different trolling plugs run best at different speeds. Some attain good action at speeds of less than 2 mph, while some speed-trolling plugs develop their best action at speeds of 5 to 7 mph. Because plug trollers usually fish with multiple lines, it's important to select lures that are compatible, meaning that they run well at the same speed.

With multiple lines, you can frequently change lures to determine the most productive color, size, action and depth. Then, you can change your lure spread accordingly.

Plug trollers rely heavily on their electronics to help them locate and stay with fish.

Besides a good depth finder, many use water-temperature and trolling-speed indicators. And once they find a school of fish in open water, they punch a waypoint into their GPS unit so they can easily find it again on the next trolling pass.

Let out cord until the board has planed out the desired distance, usually about 50 feet. The elevated mast prevents the cord from dragging in the water; otherwise the board would not plane properly.

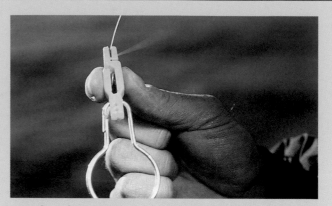

Let the plug out the desired distance (at least 100 feet in clear water) and then attach your line to a sliding release.

Continue to let out line until the release is within a foot or so of the board, then engage your reel to hold it there. Place your rod in a rod holder.

Let out a second line and attach it to a sliding release. Let it slide about halfway down the cord, then engage the reel and place the rod in a rod holder.

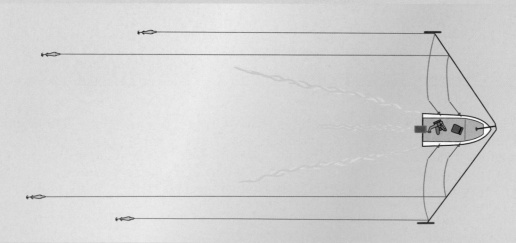

Let out the board on the opposite side of the boat and repeat the procedure. With boards out both sides of the boat, you can cover a swath of water more than 100 feet wide. When a fish strikes, it trips the release, so you can fight the fish on a free line.

Fishing with Side Planers

Let your plug out the desired distance (10 to 100 feet, depending on the depth you want to fish and water clarity), and then attach your line to a side planer.

Feed line as the planer takes your lure to the side of the boat's wake. Engage your reel when you feel the planer is far enough out and place the rod in a rod holder.

Let out additional planers on both sides of the boat to cover the desired amount of water.

When a fish strikes, reel in line until a partner can detach the planer; then you can land the fish on a free line.

Tips for Fishing with Trolling Plugs

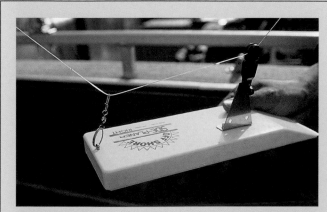

Rig your planer board to release automatically and slide down your line when a fish strikes by threading your line through a snap, as shown. Be sure to add a large barrel swivel to keep it from sliding all the way to the lure.

Use a line-counter reel when fishing with trolling plugs. This way, you can easily monitor the amount of line that is out and, should you hook a fish, easily return to the same depth. With an ordinary level-wind, count the number of passes of the level-wind guide to keep track of line length.

JERKBAITS

Large predator fish are constantly on the lookout for an easy meal, so they're quick to home in on a smaller fish that is swimming erratically. Jerkbaits take advantage of this behavior, mimicking an injured fish by diving beneath the surface and then floating up or darting wildly from side to side.

These large, wooden plugs fall into two categories: divers and gliders. Divers swoop downward when pulled forward; gliders veer to the side. Jerkbaits have no action of their own; the way they move in the water depends on how the angler works them.

Although jerkbaits are used mainly for big pike and muskies, it's not unusual for a good-sized walleye or bass to grab the bait. You can catch fish on jerkbaits throughout the open water season but, when the water temperature dips below 60°F, a glider is a better choice than a diver. Retrieve it more slowly than you would in warm water.

Because jerkbaits move so much water, they produce sounds and vibrations that are easy for gamefish to detect, even in low-clarity water or under low-light conditions. With their open hooks, they are not a good choice for fishing in dense weeds, but they can be worked over weed tops or threaded through slots in the vegetation. A diver works better than a glider for fishing slots, because it has very little lateral movement.

Jerkbaits are not a good choice in water more than 10 feet deep. Few jerkbaits run deeper than 8 feet and, if you add heavy sinkers, they won't have the proper action. Some anglers, however, add internal weights for a little extra depth or to make the bait neutrally buoyant (p. 25).

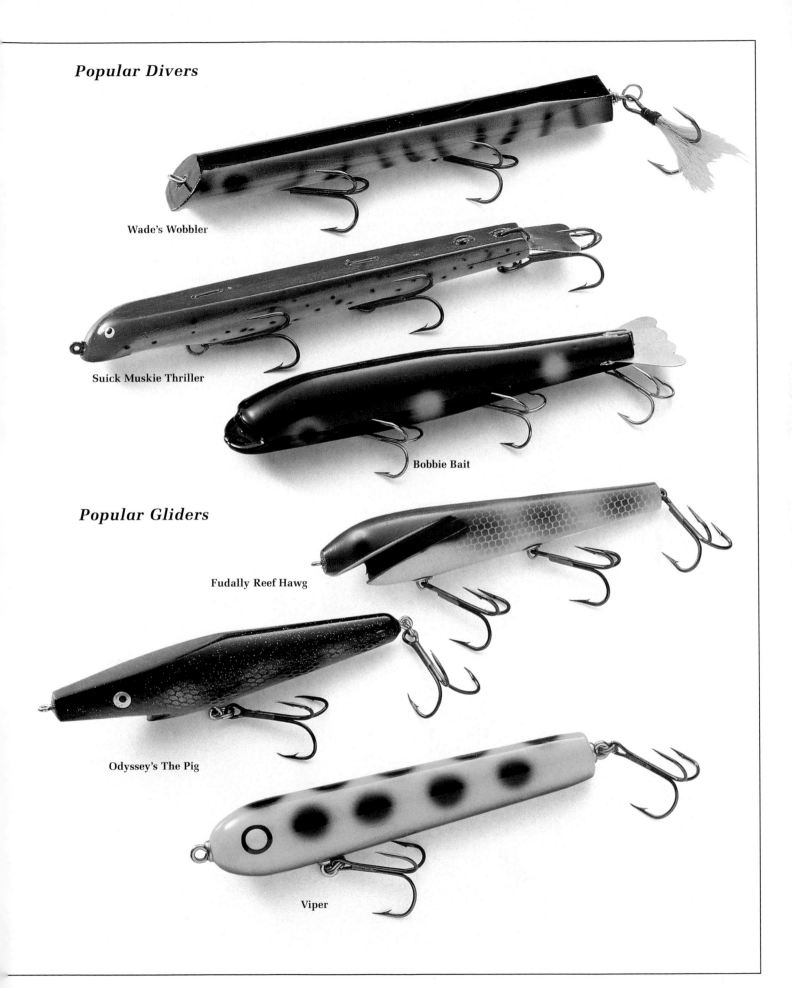

Popular Divers

Wade's Wobbler

Suick Muskie Thriller

Bobbie Bait

Popular Gliders

Fudally Reef Hawg

Odyssey's The Pig

Viper

Jerkbait Fishing

Serious pike and muskie anglers rank jerkbaits near the top of their list of favorite lures. The injured-minnow action draws strikes even when the fish are not actively feeding.

Jerkbaits are almost always fished by casting and retrieving with downward sweeps of the rod. Divers are normally retrieved with longer sweeps of the rod than gliders (below), but it pays to experiment with different sweep lengths and durations between sweeps until you discover what the fish want on a particular day.

But trolling with jerkbaits also works well. Motor slowly along a distinct weed edge or over a weedy flat while making a series of sideways sweeps of the rod.

Because the majority of jerkbaits run very shallow, normally at depths of 2 to 4 feet, many experienced anglers add weight to make them run deeper. Weighting is most commonly done with divers; not only does it increase their running depth, it makes them float up more slowly. This way, you can reduce the length of your sweeps and the duration between them without losing depth.

To weight a jerkbait, wrap solder around the hooks, add golfer's tape to the belly or implant lead sinkers into the wood and seal them in with epoxy.

One of the biggest problems in jerkbait fishing is setting the hook. Fish may have trouble zeroing in on the erratically moving bait and,

How to Retrieve Jerkbaits

Retrieve a jerkbait with smooth downward sweeps of the rod. To fish a diver, start by pointing your rod at the bait and make a long sweep, stopping the rod at 5 or 6 o'clock. Reel up slack and return the rod to its original position as the bait floats up and then give it another downward sweep. This imparts an erratic up-and-down motion to the lure (upper right). To fish a glider, start by pointing your rod at the bait and make a shorter sweep, stopping the rod at about 4 o'clock. Reel up slack before the lure finishes its glide and then make another downward sweep to make the lure change direction. This gives the lure an enticing side-to-side motion (lower right).

even when they do hit, there could be slack in your line if you're between sweeps.

Adding to the difficulty is the fact that a big pike or muskie often sinks its teeth into the wood when it grabs a jerkbait, so you can't move the lure enough to sink the hooks.

Because jerkbaiting requires a stiff, powerful rod, you must play the fish carefully. If you attempt to horse it in, there's a good chance that you'll tear out the hooks. Keep your drag tight on the hookset, but loosen it a little for playing the fish.

Most jerkbaits have three large trebles, so it's not uncommon for a fish to become so entangled in the hooks that it can't be released in good condition. This explains why many anglers carry a pair of sidecutters. Then, should a fish become badly hooked, they can simply cut off the barbs and release the fish unharmed.

Recommended Tackle

Casting and retrieving these heavy lures requires a stiff, powerful baitcasting rod no more than 6 1/2 feet long. A longer rod would slap the water on the downward sweep. A rod with an extra-long handle gives you more leverage for casting these big baits and making powerful hooksets. Use a sturdy baitcasting reel with a smooth drag and spool up with 30- to 50-pound test Dacron or superline. For pike or muskie fishing, be sure to add a heavy solid-wire or braided-wire leader.

Jerkbaiting Tips

Weight a diver so it floats level, with its back just breaking the surface. A bait weighted this way will run several feet deeper than it otherwise would.

Some divers have metal tails that can be bent slightly downward to make them dive deeper.

A wire leader inhibits the action of a glider, but you can improve the side-to-side movement by adding a split ring between the clip and the attachment eye.

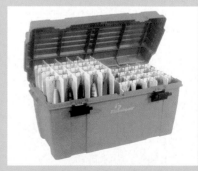

Carry your jerkbaits in a specially designed tackle box, such as a Flambeau Maximizer, that protects the hooks. Some anglers use a styrofoam cooler, but this leaves the hooks exposed.

MAGNUM BASS PLUGS

These lures defy classification, but they all have one thing in common: they're big. Most measure at least 10 inches in length and some are as long as 15.

Many of these lures were designed by California anglers who were trying to find lures big enough to tempt giant Florida bass, which are known to be fond of stocked rainbow trout. But the lures have found many applications for other large gamefish species, including striped bass, muskies and lake trout.

The majority of these lures are made of wood. Some have a flexible rubber tail, which gives them a realistic swimming action. Not surprisingly, the most popular color is rainbow trout, although they come in other colors as well.

One reason these baits attract big fish is that their wide wobble results in a low-frequency vibration, which replicates that produced by a good-sized baitfish. This means that gamefish can easily identify the bait as a desirable food item from a distance, even in water where it's not possible to see it.

Magnum bass plugs can be fished by casting or trolling. Because of their large size, it takes a fairly rapid retrieve to generate the best action, although some anglers fish them slowly on the surface.

Like crankbaits, these lures work best when allowed to periodically bump logs, rocks or other cover, or tick the bottom to interrupt the action.

Although magnum bass plugs are proven big-fish baits, don't plan on finding a large selection at your local tackle shop. Many of these lures are produced by hand by local anglers and sell for more than $50 each. Some major manufacturers, however, have started to mass-produce baits of this type.

Recommended Tackle

Magnum bass plugs may weigh more than a quarter-pound, so it takes a long, stiff rod to cast them. Many anglers prefer a 7 1/2-foot, heavy-power, fast-action flippin' stick, but some favor a 7-foot muskie rod or a light surfcasting rod. Because these lures pull so hard, they're easiest to fish with a baitcasting reel that has a gear ratio no greater than 5:1. It should be spooled with 20- to 30-pound-test mono.

A.C. Plug

Z-Plug

Jack's Whacker

Castaic Trout Lure

TOPWATER LURES

*N*othing in freshwater fishing matches the thrill of a topwater strike. But there's another reason for the popularity of topwater lures: They catch lots of fish.

TOPWATER LURES

It's easy to understand why so many anglers get hooked on topwater fishing. No other form of angling is as visual – you actually see the fish take the lure.

Some topwater lures imitate injured minnows; others, frogs, rats, mice or even large insects. But what the lure looks like is much less important to the fish than its action and the sound it produces. Most topwaters make a gurgling, spluttering, chugging or popping sound, but some barely disturb the surface, making no sound at all.

Although surface feeding fish will take most any kind of lure that floats, the following types of lures are intended solely for topwater fishing:

- **Stickbaits** - These long, thin plugs are weighted in the tail, so they "walk" from side to side when retrieved with a series of twitches.
- **Propbaits** - These plugs resemble stickbaits, but they have propellers at one or both ends and are not weighted in the tail. They have a sputtering action when fished with a twitch-and-pause retrieve.
- **Chuggers** - With their flattened or dished face, these plugs make a popping sound and throw water when given a sharp twitch.
- **Crawlers** - A wide face plate or arms give these plugs a crawling action that produces a gurgling sound.
- **Frogs & Rats** - Made of soft rubber or plastic, these lures usually have weedless hooks, so they work well in heavy vegetation. Some have legs that produce a kicking action while others barely make a ripple.
- **Buzzbaits** - A large blade throws water when the lure is reeled steadily across the surface. If you stop reeling, the lure sinks.

Topwater Selection Guide

Fish Species	Lure Length
Smallmouth and spotted bass	2-4 inches
Northern largemouth bass	2-6 inches
Florida largemouth bass	4-8 inches
Northern pike, muskie and striper	6-12 inches

Frog

Buzzbait

Rat

Chugger

Stickbait

Crawler

Propbait

BUZZBAITS

A buzzbait is an excellent "locator" lure; you can cast it a long way and retrieve it rapidly to draw strikes that reveal the whereabouts of gamefish. Once you've located the fish, you can switch to a slower presentation to put more of them in the boat.

Buzzbaits will catch most any surface-feeding gamefish, but they're most popular with largemouth bass anglers. And giant buzzbaits have recently started to gain favor among pike and muskie addicts.

With its large, double- or triple-winged *buzzblade*, a buzzbait creates more surface disturbance than most other topwaters. The blade turns on a straight-wire or safety-pin shaft, producing an intense gurgling action that attracts fish even in murky water. Some buzzbaits have a pair of counter-rotating blades that create even more commotion.

A buzzbait with a safety-pin shaft is the best choice for fishing in weedy or brushy cover. The shaft, like that of a spinnerbait, runs interference for the upturned hook, preventing it from fouling or hanging up.

Some in-line buzzers have a treble hook instead of a single. They work well in snag-free cover, because they give you a better hooking percentage.

Like other topwaters, buzzbaits should be tied directly to your line, unless you're fishing pike or muskies. A heavy leader or clip will sink the nose, preventing the blade from spinning.

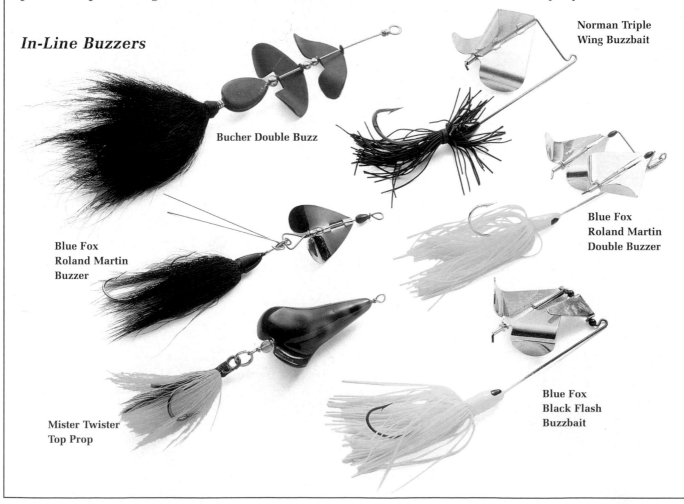

In-Line Buzzers

Bucher Double Buzz

Blue Fox Roland Martin Buzzer

Mister Twister Top Prop

Safety-Pin Buzzers

Norman Triple Wing Buzzbait

Blue Fox Roland Martin Double Buzzer

Blue Fox Black Flash Buzzbait

How to Retrieve a Buzzbait

Make a long cast and start your retrieve with your rod tip high. This keeps the bait riding high in the water so the blade can spin freely.

Gradually lower the rod tip as the bait approaches the boat. Keeping the rod tip high would pull the bait out of the water so the blade wouldn't spin.

Four Buzzbaiting Tips

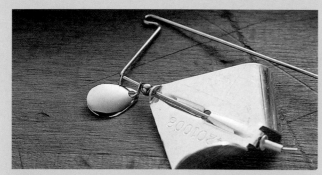

Add a "clacker" blade for extra attraction. Remove the buzzblade, slide some beads and a clevis with a small Colorado blade onto the upper arm and then replace the buzzblade. When the buzzblade turns, it will clack against the Colorado blade.

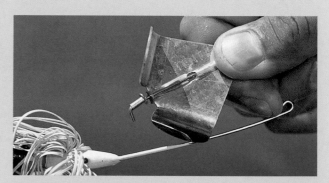

Bend the shaft slightly so the blade barely ticks the arm as it spins. The extra noise often makes a big difference.

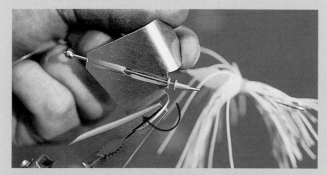

Buzzbaits do not work well when retrieved slowly, because the blade won't spin. But you can solve the problem by cupping the blades, as shown, to make them catch more water. The more you cup the blades, the slower you can retrieve.

Drill several holes in each wing of a buzzblade, causing it to leave a trail of bubbles when you retrieve. The bubbles make it easier for fish to track the bait.

CRAWLERS

Of all the topwaters, crawlers are the easiest to fish because all you have to do is cast them out and reel them in. And, because they can be retrieved quite rapidly, crawlers are excellent "locator" lures.

Crawlers produce an enticing gurgle that draws the attention of any surface feeding gamefish. This sound, along with the predictable action, explains why crawlers are so effective for night fishing. While fish may have trouble zeroing in on a lure moving erratically, they have no trouble tracking one with a steady action.

Some of these lures get their crawling action from a broad, cupped face plate; others, from arms at the sides of the body. Models with arms usually have a more-intense action than those with face plates.

Because of their open hooks, crawlers are not a good choice for fishing in weedy cover. Face-plate models work well in sparse weeds, but models with arms tend to collect sprigs of vegetation.

The only variable in fishing a crawler is the speed of the retrieve. Every model has a certain speed at which it works best. If your retrieve is too fast, the lure will skitter across the water with practically no action. If it's too slow, the lure won't wobble enough or produce the gurgling sound.

Although a steady retrieve will normally draw the most strikes, there are times when the fish prefer a stop-and-go or twitch-and-pause retrieve.

Tie a crawler directly to your line or attach it with a small clip. A crawler's balance is not as critical as that of most other topwaters, but try to avoid weighting down the nose with a heavy leader or snap-swivel.

Recommended Tackle

Long casts are important in crawler fishing, so you'll want a fairly long rod. A 7- to 7 1/2-foot, medium-heavy-power baitcaster with an extra-long handle for two-handed casting is ideal. Pair this with a high-speed baitcasting reel spooled with 12- to 17-pound-test monofilament.

How to use a Crawler as a "Locator" Lure

Fancast a large, weedy flat using a crawler (left). Retrieve at a fairly rapid rate and note the exact location of any boils or short strikes (right). Try another cast or two with the crawler and then, if the fish doesn't strike, switch to a "slower" subsurface lure, such as a jig or plastic worm, and thoroughly work the area where you saw the boil. The slower presentation will often trigger a strike.

Popular Crawlers

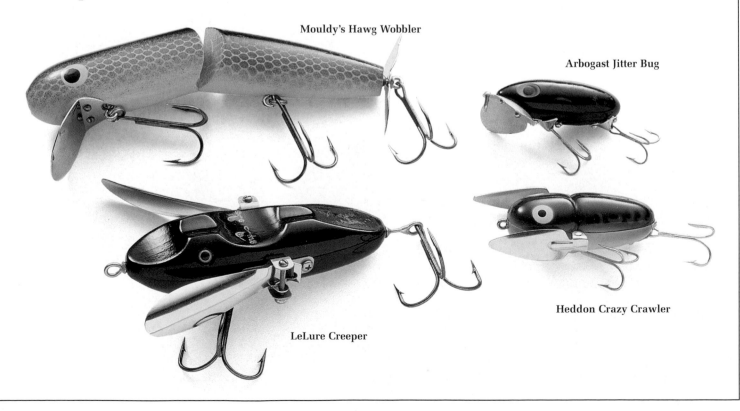

Mouldy's Hawg Wobbler

Arbogast Jitter Bug

LeLure Creeper

Heddon Crazy Crawler

STICKBAITS

When retrieved properly, a stickbait has an erratic, side-to-side action that gamefish evidently mistake for a crippled minnow. In clear water, it's not uncommon for a stickbait to "call up" fish from depths of 20 feet.

Stickbaits are known as big-fish lures. For decades, they have been popular for largemouth, smallmouth and spotted bass, but anglers are now discovering that larger models work equally well for northern pike, muskies and striped bass.

Most stickbaits are made of hollow plastic and have an internal lead weight near the tail, so they float with their head up. This allows for the free lateral head movement necessary for the side-to-side retrieve called "walking the dog" (below).

The key to getting the right action from a stickbait is learning to throw slack into the line after each downward stroke of the rod. If you keep the line taut, the lure will not scoot to the side as far as it should and you will not get a sharp enough twitch on the next stroke.

Stickbaits don't throw a lot of water and their action is less intense than that of most other topwaters, so they work best in water that is relatively clear and calm. They're ideal for calling fish up out of submerged weed beds, but they're not a good choice for fishing in emergent vegetation, because their lateral action causes them to hang up on the stems.

Recommended Tackle

Use a fast-action baitcasting rod no more than 6 1/2 feet long for walking the dog. A longer rod will slap the water on the downward stroke, and a rod with a soft tip will not give you the sharp twitches necessary to make the lure change direction. Ten- to 14-pound mono is adequate for most stickbait fishing but, for pike, muskies and stripers, use 17- to 20-pound mono.

Walking the Dog

Retrieve a stickbait by pointing your rod directly at the lure, giving it a sharp downward stroke and then stopping it at 5 or 6 o'clock (left). Immediately after completing the downward stroke, lift your rod to throw slack into the line. This way, the lure will dart sharply to the side (upper right). After the lure completes its sideways glide, give it another sharp jerk and throw slack into the line to make it dart the opposite way (lower right).

Artificial Lures

Popular Stickbaits

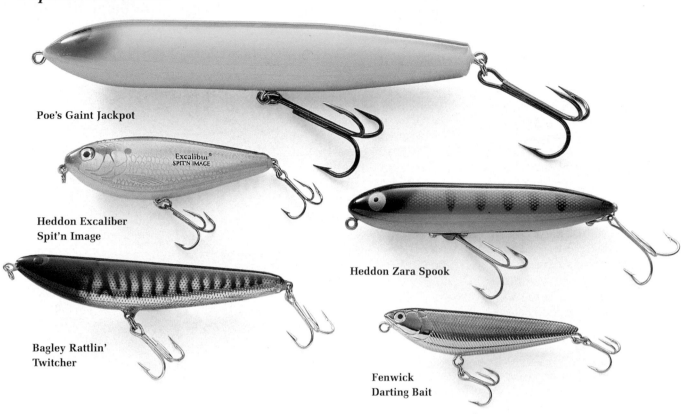

Poe's Gaint Jackpot

Heddon Excaliber Spit'n Image

Bagley Rattlin' Twitcher

Heddon Zara Spook

Fenwick Darting Bait

The lateral action also makes it difficult for fish to home in on the bait, so you'll experience a fair number of missed strikes. But you can improve your hooking percentage by pausing until you feel the weight of the fish before setting the hook.

Unless you're fishing for pike or muskies, tie your stickbait directly to your line. Heavy snaps or leaders inhibit the side-to-side action.

Tips for Fishing with Stickbaits

If your stickbait has "old-style" hook hangers (left), replace them with screw eyes and split rings (right). This way, the hooks can move more freely, making it more difficult for fish to throw the lure.

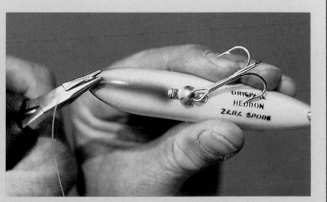

To make your lure veer to one side, bend the attachment eye to the opposite side. This makes it possible to work the bait under a dock or other overhead cover.

PROPBAITS

Gamefish can't help but notice the sputtering action of a propbait, even in choppy or discolored water. While some propbaits have small blades that throw only a little water, others have huge blades that churn the water violently.

The majority of propbaits have propellers at both ends, but some have blades at one end or the other. In a number of large propbaits, the blade is affixed to the head or tail, so that entire part of the body spins. This creates more surface disturbance than a propeller alone.

Propbaits resemble stickbaits and are used for the same species of gamefish, but they are retrieved somewhat differently. Because most propbaits have no tail weight, they do not work well for a walk-the-dog retrieve. Instead, they are normally fished with a straight twitch-and-pause retrieve. Vary the length of your twitches and the duration of your pauses until you find the combination that works best for the conditions.

Accomplished propbait fishermen know how to work the lure very slowly so the blades throw water without the lure moving ahead too much. The secret is twitching it sharply on a slack line.

There are times, however, when a steady retrieve may work better. When the fish are active, they may grab a steadily moving bait to prevent it from getting away.

Like stickbaits, propbaits should be tied directly to the line. A heavy leader or snap weights down the nose, preventing the front propeller from throwing water. For pike or muskie fishing, attach a short wire leader to prevent bite-offs.

Twin-Blade Propbaits

Cisco Kid Topper

Smithwick
Devil's Horse

Cordell Crazy Shad

Tips for Using Propbaits

Blow on the propellers to make sure they spin easily. If they do not, try bending the blades backward or forward or twisting them to change their pitch.

Recommended Tackle

A medium-heavy power, fast-action baitcasting rod from 6½ to 7 feet in length is ideal for propbait fishing. For pike or muskie fishing, or for propbaits with a front propeller, use 17- to 20-pound mono; lighter line is too limp and may catch on the blade. Twelve- to 14-pound mono is usually adequate for lures with only a rear propeller.

Single-Blade Propbaits

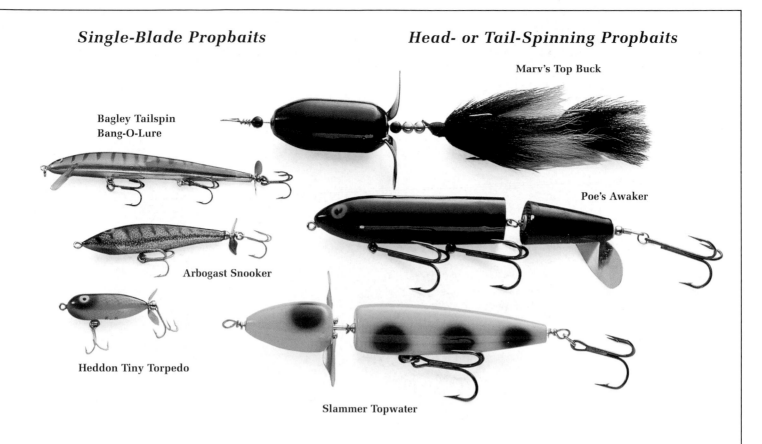

Single-Blade Propbaits

Bagley Tailspin
Bang-O-Lure

Arbogast Snooker

Heddon Tiny Torpedo

Head- or Tail-Spinning Propbaits

Marv's Top Buck

Poe's Awaker

Slammer Topwater

Bend the propeller blades forward, as shown, to catch finicky gamefish. Bending the blades this way reduces the distance the bait moves forward when you twitch it.

Be alert for a bulge just behind your propbait; it's the back of a fish that is following the lure. Resist the tendency to slow down. Instead, reel faster to entice the fish to strike.

FROGS & RATS

Topwater frogs are among the earliest of artificial lures. And the fact that they've survived so long is no accident; they're one of the most effective baits for drawing bass out of dense, weedy cover.

Topwater rats resemble frogs, but they do not have legs. Although they are not as popular as frogs, they are no less effective.

These lures are hard to beat for working large expanses of matted weeds, such as beds of lily pads with a mixture of other weeds and moss. They also work well in matted-out hydrilla or milfoil. Most other surface lures would foul in this type of cover, but a frog or rat will slide right over the top.

Frogs and rats are made of foam rubber or hollow plastic. Some are extremely life-like; others bear only a vague resemblance to the real

Popular Frogs & Rats

Snag Proof Moss Mouse

Mann's Skirted Frog

Snag Proof Tournament Frog

thing. Many frogs come with pliable legs that have a kicking action when retrieved with a twitching motion.

Practically all topwater frogs and rats have upturned hooks or some type of weed-

guard, so they can be worked through the heaviest surface vegetation. Some have no built-in hooks and are designed to be Texas-rigged on an ordinary worm hook.

Recommended Tackle

Because they are normally fished in heavy cover, frogs and rats require heavy tackle. A 7 1/2-foot flippin' stick and a baitcasting reel spooled with 20- to 30-pound abrasion-resistant mono or superline makes an ideal setup. The fish are usually buried in dense weeds, so they don't notice the heavy line.

How to Retrieve Frogs & Rats

Make a long cast over a bed of matted vegetation and keep your rod tip high while drawing the frog into an open pocket.

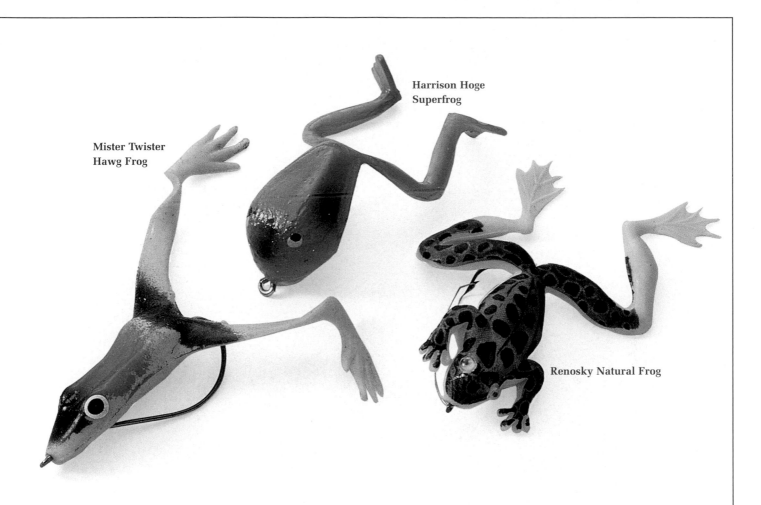

**Mister Twister
Hawg Frog**

**Harrison Hoge
Superfrog**

Renosky Natural Frog

Because of their pliable bodies, frogs and rats feel like real food. So when a bass grabs the lure, it's not likely to let go. This gives the angler a little longer to set the hook than if he were using a hard bait.

Frogs and rats are primarily hot-weather baits, because that's when bass seek out matted surface weeds, which keep the water below a few degrees cooler than the surrounding water.

When the bait reaches an open pocket, hesitate for a few seconds until all the ripples subside. Then, continue reeling until it reaches another pocket.

Cut a slit in a frog or rat and insert a rattle for extra casting weight.

CHUGGERS

Also called poppers, these lures have a concave, grooved or flattened face that makes a popping or chugging sound and throws water when the lure is given a sharp twitch.

Chuggers most closely imitate a kicking frog, so it's not surprising that they work so well for largemouth, small-mouth and spotted bass. Noisy chuggers up to a foot long are highly effective for stripers tearing into schools of shad on the surface, and small chuggers are proven white bass producers. Although a chugger will occasionally take a pike or muskie, it usually doesn't work as well as a stickbait or propbait.

A chugger can be retrieved with a series of nonstop twitches, with twitches followed by short pauses or with twitches followed by pauses long enough to allow all the ripples to subside.

Nonstop twitches enable you to cover a lot of water in a short time and are most appealing to active fish. Long

How to Retrieve a Chugger

To retrieve a chugger with a series of nonstop twitches, make a cast and then start twitching your rod while holding it at a 45-degree angle to prevent the line from sinking. As the lure approaches the boat, keep twitching while gradually lowering the rod. If you kept the rod high, you'd lift the face of the bait too much so it wouldn't throw water.

To fish a pocket in the weeds, twitch the lure and then wait for the ripples to die before twitching it again. Some anglers pause for up to a minute after the twitch.

Give the lure an explosive twitch when fishing for pack-feeding stripers or white bass. These fish are extremely aggressive feeders and the intense action gets their attention.

Artificial Lures

pauses are ideal for working pockets in the cover. When the lure reaches a likely-looking opening, give it a sharp twitch and wait several seconds for the ripples to die; that's when the fish usually strike.

Let the fish dictate how hard you twitch your popper. Sometimes they prefer subtle twitches that barely disturb the water; other times, they favor sharper jerks. Only rarely will you catch fish by jerking so hard that the lure makes a loud splash; that

much commotion usually spooks the fish.

Always attach a chugger by tying it directly to your line; if you weight down the nose

with a heavy snap or clip, the face of the lure will catch too much water when you twitch, ruining the action.

> ### Recommended Tackle
>
> A 6½-foot medium-power, medium-action baitcasting rod is a good choice for fishing chuggers, because it flexes enough to allow pinpoint casting with these lures, many of which are relatively light. Pair this with a narrow-spool, high-speed baitcasting reel, which enables you to make a rapid twitching retrieve. Spool up with 12- to 20-pound-test mono.

Popular Chuggers

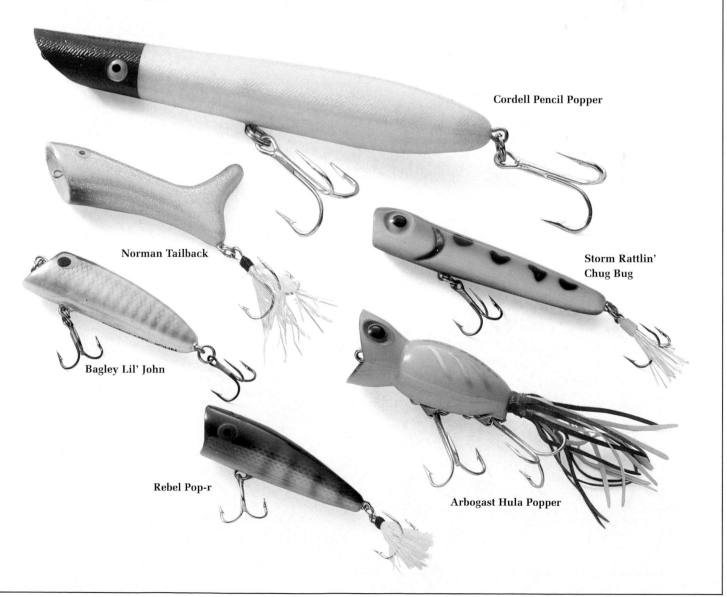

Cordell Pencil Popper

Norman Tailback

Storm Rattlin' Chug Bug

Bagley Lil' John

Bagley Lil' John

Rebel Pop-r

Arbogast Hula Popper

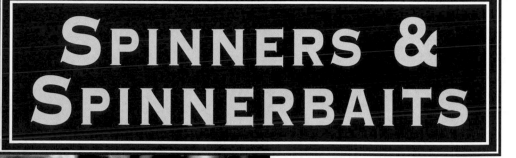

SPINNERS & SPINNERBAITS

Spinners and spinnerbaits offer a combination of flash and vibration that appeals to practically every type of gamefish that swims in fresh water.

SPINNERS & SPINNERBAITS

Spinners are one of the few lures that enjoy *worldwide* popularity, and it's easy to understand why. The spinning blade produces intense vibrations that are easily detected by a fish's lateral-line system, and the vivid flash adds a visual stimulus.

As a result, spinners work well in clear or discolored water.

Practically any kind of freshwater gamefish will strike a spinner. And the lures are equally effective in warm or cool water. The spinning blades provide plen-

ty of lift, so you can retrieve very slowly when frigid water slows fish activity.

Another reason for the popularity of spinners: they're very easy to use. They work well with a straight retrieve and, when a fish strikes, it usually hooks itself.

There are two basic types of spinners: in-line spinners and spinnerbaits. The blade of an in-line spinner rotates around a straight-wire shaft with a hook at the rear. A spinnerbait has a safety-pin-style shaft with the spinner blade(s) attached to the upper arm and a weighted head and single hook on the lower arm.

Spinnerbait

One of the main considerations in selecting a spinner is the blade shape. Colorado, Indiana and willow-leaf blades make up the majority of the market, although there are many other types with slightly different shapes. Each of these blade types varies in the amount of lift it generates and the amount of vibration it produces.

In-line spinner

Anglers should also pay close attention to blade size. Blades come in sizes 00 (the smallest) to 7 (the largest). Small blades rotate faster, so they produce high-frequency vibrations that gamefish identify as the rapid tail movement of a small baitfish. Larger blades have a lower frequency and simulate the slower movement of a larger baitfish.

Blade-Size Guide

Fish Species	Blade Size
Crappie, sunfish, perch, small trout	00 to 1
White bass	0 to 2
Smallmouth and spotted bass	1 to 3
Northern largemouth bass, walleye	2 to 4
Large trout and salmon	3 to 6
Northern pike, muskie, striper and Florida largemouth bass	4 to 7

Blade Styles & Sizes

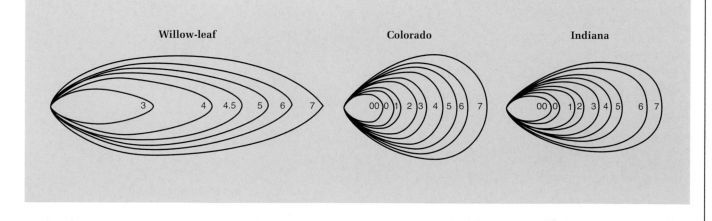

Willow-leaf   Colorado   Indiana

In-Line Spinners

Ask a seasoned trout angler to name the best "hardware" for stream trout and he's likely to say the in-line spinner. Ask a veteran muskie fisherman to divulge his favorite artificial and you'll probably get the same answer. Not only are in-line spinners effective on a wide variety of gamefish, they rank among the top-rated lures for many of them.

Here are the main types of in-line spinners:

- "French" spinners, which are small to medium in size and usually have a sparse hook dressing or no dressing at all.
- Bucktails, which are large spinners used mainly for pike and muskies. They have bushy deer-hair or synthetic-fiber tails that give the bait an attractive billowing action.
- Weight-forward spinners, which are the only type that has the weight in front of the blade.
- Sonic spinners, which have a blade that is concave on one end and convex on the other, so the blade turns very easily and will spin at a very slow retrieve speed.

In the other types of in-line spinners, the blade rotates around the shaft on a clevis, which is a small metal or plastic attachment device. But in sonic spinners, the shaft fits through a hole in the blade; there is no clevis.

In-line spinners are used mainly in water that is relatively free of obstructions. They are not a good choice in heavy cover. If you try retrieving them through dense vegetation, weed fragments will foul the open hooks and stop the blade from turning.

If tied directly to your line, in-line spinners will cause excessive line twist. Be sure to attach these lures with a snap-swivel, preferably the ball-bearing type.

On the pages that follow, we'll explain how to use each type of in-line spinner and offer some tips for making these lures more effective.

Types of In-Line Spinners

Bucktail (Blue Fox Musky Buck)

Weight-forward (Erie Dearie)

French (Mepps Aglia)

Sonic (Panther Martin)

French & Sonic Spinners

These spinners are a natural for stream fishing, because even slowly moving water causes the small blade to spin. This means that you can "hang" the lure in the current, letting it flutter in the face of fish holding behind a boulder or other cover. And by changing your rod position, you can present the bait to various fish lies without having to cast.

In lakes, these lures can be fished over rocky points, gravelly shoals, weed tops or other shallow cover. Or they can be counted down to fish weed edges, humps or other deeper structure.

French and sonic spinners are normally fished with a slow, steady retrieve. The trick is reeling just fast enough to make the blades turn. But some anglers prefer to fish these baits with a lift-and-drop retrieve, much like you would fish a jig.

When you're fishing in discolored water, a French spinner is usually a better choice than a sonic spinner, because the blade vibrations are more intense. These strong vibra-

A sonic spinner is a top stream-trout lure.

tions also mean that fish can detect a French spinner from a greater distance.

Popular French & Sonic Spinners

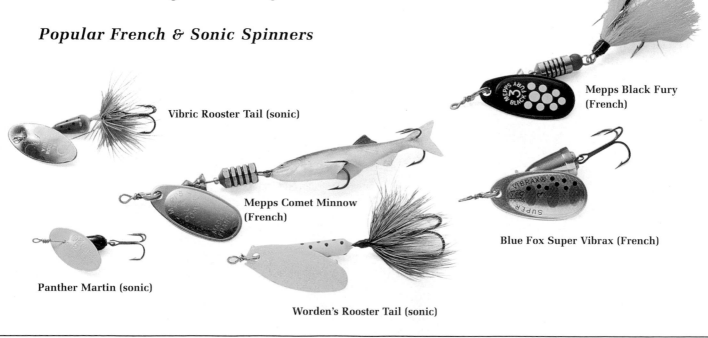

Vibric Rooster Tail (sonic)

Mepps Black Fury (French)

Mepps Comet Minnow (French)

Blue Fox Super Vibrax (French)

Panther Martin (sonic)

Worden's Rooster Tail (sonic)

Weight-Forward Spinners

Weight-forward spinners differ from other types of inline spinners in that the positioning of the weight causes the blade to turn while the lure is sinking headfirst. As a result, these lures are ideal for catching suspended fish using the "countdown technique."

The method is simple. Just make a long cast and count while the lure is sinking. Start your retrieve on different counts until you determine the best depth, and then continue counting down to that level.

Most weight-forward spinners are weighted quite heavily, so they can be cast long distances. This explains their popularity with big-water anglers who need to cover a lot of water to find the fish. Weight-forward spinners are also a good choice for fishing in fast current because they hold their depth so well.

Weight-forward spinners are usually tipped with a

Big walleyes find it hard to resist a weight-forward spinner and a crawler.

Popular Weight-Forward Spinners

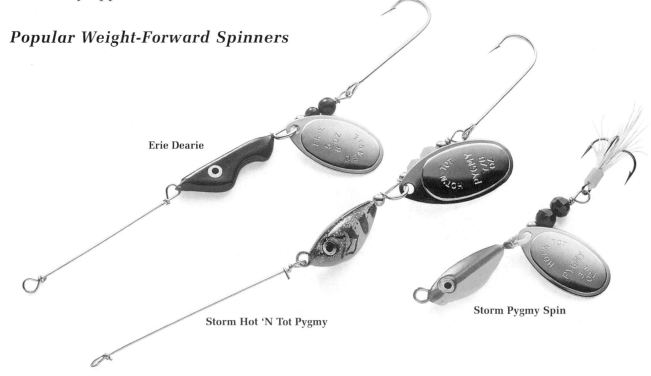

Erie Dearie

Storm Hot 'N Tot Pygmy

Storm Pygmy Spin

nightcrawler, minnow or some other type of live bait. They can also be tipped with pork rind or a soft-plastic grub. Most models come with a single hook that rides with the point up to minimize snagging and fouling.

Unlike other types of in-line spinners, weight-forward spinners aren't likely to twist your line. In most models, the weight acts as a keel, preventing the lure from spinning. Consequently, there is no need to use a snap-swivel; just tie your line directly to the lure.

Recommended Tackle

A medium- to medium-heavy-power, long-handled baitcasting rod from 6 1/2 to 7 feet in length works well for distance casting with weight-forward spinners. For maximum casting distance, use a wide-spool baitcasting reel spooled with 8- to 12-pound-test monofilament.

How to Fish a Weight-Forward Spinner

Tip a weight-forward spinner by hooking a crawler several times, so only about an inch of the tail is trailing. Hook a minnow by pushing the hook through the mouth, out the gill and into the back.

Lob cast with a sidearm motion to avoid tearing off the bait and to prevent the hook from catching the line. Because the lure sails headfirst, the hook tangles easily, especially if you snap-cast.

2 count
4 count
6 count
8 count
10 count
12 count
14 count
16 count
18 count

Count the lure down to different depths to locate the fish, and then stick with that count. Here, the angler failed to catch fish on counts of 6, 8 and 10. He began catching them on a count of 12 and found the most fish at a count of 14.

Bucktails

Big pike and muskies find it hard to resist the "breathing" action of a bucktail spinner. As the bait tracks through the water, the rippling hair creates an ultrarealistic look.

At water temperatures of 60°F or below, try a 4- or 5-inch bucktail; above 60, use a 6- to 12-incher. Small bucktails usually come with a single dressed treble hook, but larger ones usually have two in-line trebles.

Bucktails can be used in sparse weeds but, because of their open hooks, do not work well in heavy vegetation. There, a spinnerbait (p. 54) would be much better choice.

How deep a bucktail runs depends on the amount of dressing, the bait's weight and the type of blade. For maximum depth, select a heavily weighted, sparsely dressed bait with a willow-leaf blade.

Recommended Tackle

A typical "bucktail" rod is about 7 1/2 feet long with a fast action and a long handle for extra casting leverage. The long rod not only makes casting easier, it helps you guide the lure through slots in the weeds and "bulge" it on the surface. The rod should be paired with a sturdy baitcasting reel spooled with 30- to 50-pound-test Dacron or superline. Bucktails are usually fished on a solid-wire leader.

Popular Bucktail Spinners

Blue Fox Musky Buck

Buchertail

Windel's Harasser

Mepps Giant Killer

Bend the shaft of an in-line spinner, as shown, to eliminate line twist.

Angle your casts upstream when fishing a spinner in current. If you cast cross-stream or downstream, the current will create too much water resistance and cause the lure to break water.

Trim the hair on a bucktail to reduce the bait's buoyancy. This way, the bait will stay deep, even when you're "burning" it (reeling rapidly) to draw strikes.

Hang a spinner in the current and move your rod tip to fish boulders, logs and other visible cover without moving your feet.

Figure-eight a bucktail when you see a muskie or pike following it. With a foot of line out, plunge your rod tip as deep as you can and pull the bait in a large, slow figure-eight pattern. Make sure your reel is in free-spool and your thumb is on the spool. That way, you can easily feed line should a fish strike.

SPINNERBAITS

The spinnerbait is arguably the most versatile of all artificial lures. You can run it through dense weeds, bulge it on the surface, slow-roll it over brushy cover, helicopter it down a steep break or jig it along the bottom. No other lure lends itself to so many retrieves and such a variety of cover types.

Although spinnerbaits are known mainly as bass lures, they're also used for catching pike, muskies, pickerel, crappies, sunfish and even walleyes.

The design of a spinnerbait is nothing less than ingenious. The safety-pin shaft runs interference for the blade and upturned hook, and the weighted, bullet-shaped head provides stability, so the lure won't tip or twist.

Hundreds of models are available, but there are just three basic styles: the single-spin, the tandem-spin and the twin-spin (right).

Besides the blade configuration, here are some other considerations in selecting spinnerbaits:

- **Length of Upper Arm** - Most spinnerbaits are designed so the blade rides directly above the hook point. That way, when a fish strikes at the blade, it usually gets hooked. But a spinnerbait with a shorter-than-normal upper arm works better for helicoptering and, because it produces intense vibrations, is a good choice for fishing at night or in muddy water. However, the arm should not be so short that it doesn't protect the hook.

- **Shaft Thickness** - For the best action, your spinnerbait should have a thin-wire shaft that transmits the blade vibrations to the skirt, giving it a shimmering, lifelike appearance. And a thin-wire shaft bends inward when a fish strikes, upping your hooking percentage. But the constant bending fatigues most thin-wire shafts, causing them to weaken and eventually break. Titanium shafts solve the problem. They transmit vibrations extremely well, and can be bent repeatedly without weakening.

- **Type of Skirt** - Most spinnerbait skirts are made of live-rubber or silicone. Silicone skirts are a good choice in clear water; the clear or translucent material has a lifelike look. Rubber

A titanium shaft is virtually unbreakable.

skirts work better in murky water, because they produce more vibration.

You can also buy spinnerbaits with hair, feather, vinyl, tinsel or mylar skirts. Some skirts are made of a combination of these materials.

Some spinnerbaits, called spin-rigs, have no skirt at all. They're intended to be tipped with live bait or a pork trailer.

- **Blade style** - Like other types of spinners, spinnerbaits are made with Colorado, willow-leaf and

Short-arm spinnerbait

Popular Trailers

Pork eel

Pork frog

Plastic frog

Curlytail grubs

Indiana blades, with the first two being the most common. Colorado blades provide the most lift and vibration and are best for helicoptering. Willow-leaf blades have much less lift and vibration, but produce a lot of flash. Many tandem-spins have a large willow-leaf blade and a small Colorado.

For extra attraction, many anglers tip their spinnerbaits with some type of trailer. A bulky trailer also gives the lure more buoyancy, so you can easily keep it above the weed tops.

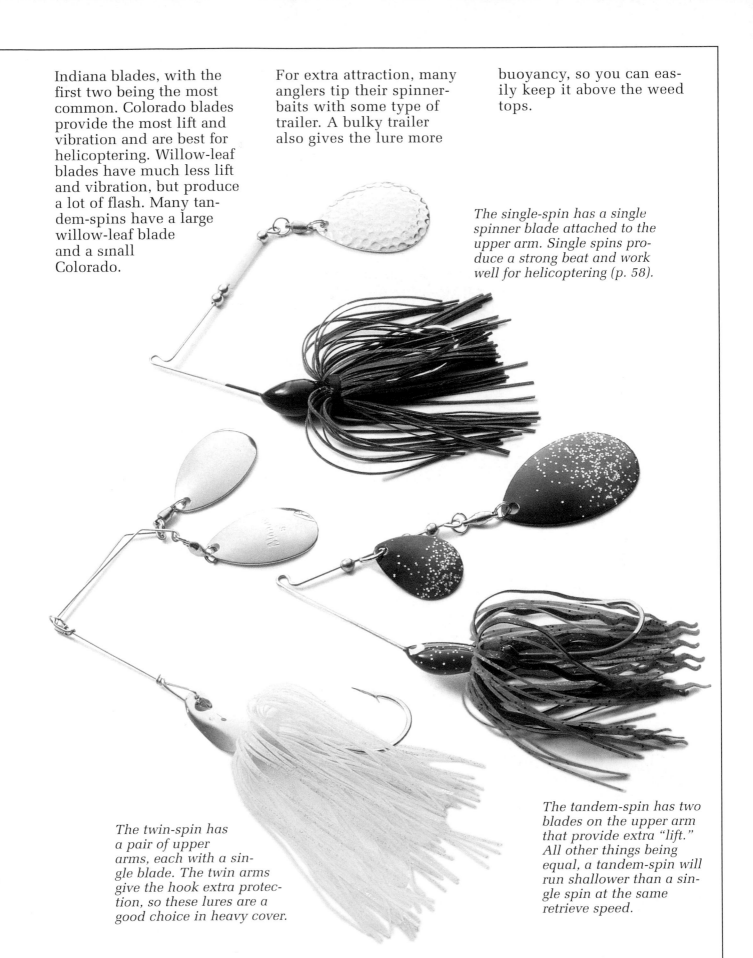

The single-spin has a single spinner blade attached to the upper arm. Single spins produce a strong beat and work well for helicoptering (p. 58).

The twin-spin has a pair of upper arms, each with a single blade. The twin arms give the hook extra protection, so these lures are a good choice in heavy cover.

The tandem-spin has two blades on the upper arm that provide extra "lift." All other things being equal, a tandem-spin will run shallower than a single spin at the same retrieve speed.

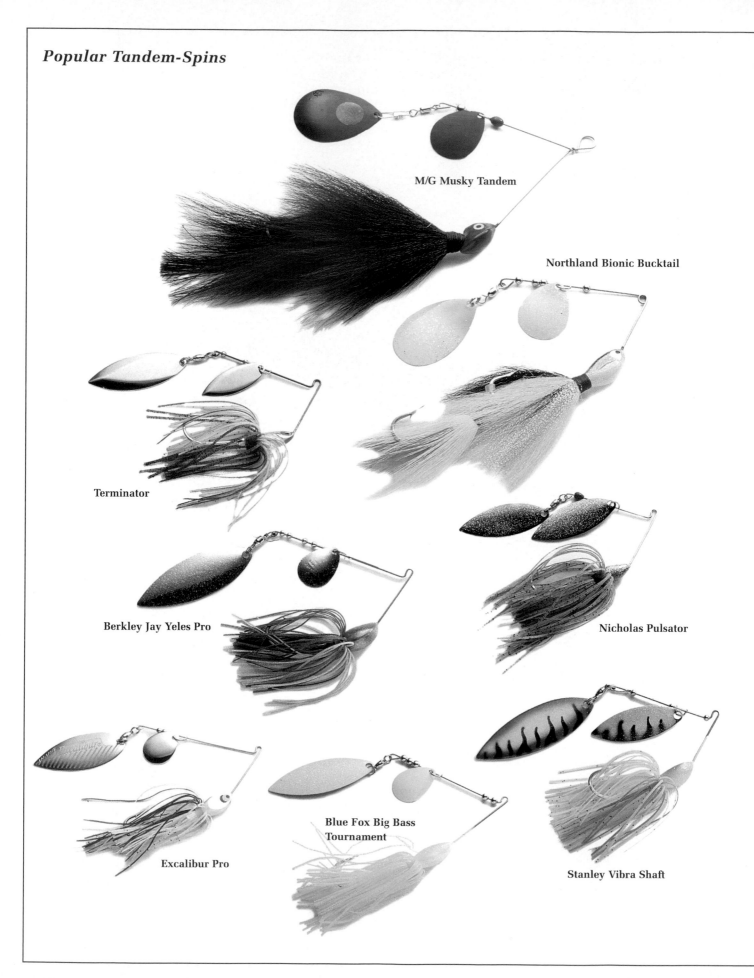

M/G Musky Tandem

Northland Bionic Bucktail

Terminator

Berkley Jay Yeles Pro

Nicholas Pulsator

Excalibur Pro

Blue Fox Big Bass Tournament

Stanley Vibra Shaft

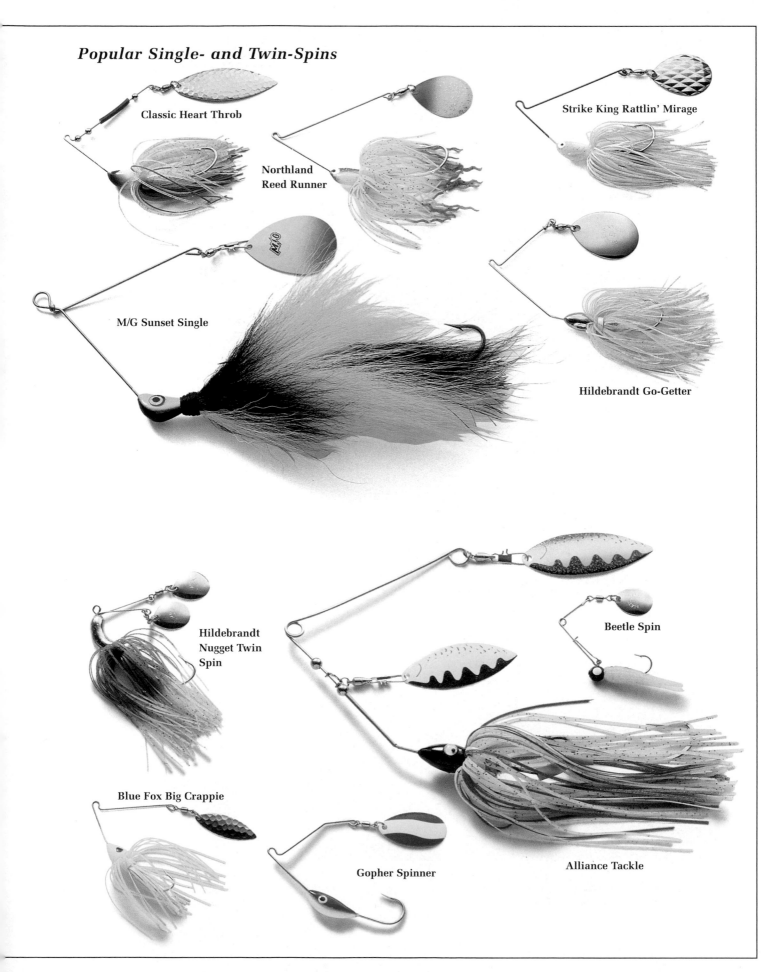

Popular Single- and Twin-Spins

Classic Heart Throb

Northland Reed Runner

Strike King Rattlin' Mirage

M/G Sunset Single

Hildebrandt Go-Getter

Hildebrandt Nugget Twin Spin

Beetle Spin

Blue Fox Big Crappie

Gopher Spinner

Alliance Tackle

How to Fish Spinnerbaits

All you have to do to catch fish on a spinnerbait is toss it out and reel it in. But spinnerbait specialists know that fine-tuning your presentation to suit the conditions will produce a lot more fish.

The first step is selecting a spinnerbait of the proper size. For crappies and sunfish, you'll want a ¹/₃₂- to ¹/₈-ounce spinnerbait; for smallmouth and spotted bass, ¹/₈ to ³/₈ ounce; for largemouth bass and small to medium northern pike, ¹/₄ to 1 ounce; for walleye, ¹/₈ to ¹/₂ ounce (spin-rig) and for large northern pike and muskies, up to 3 ounces.

The retrieves shown on these pages will catch fish in the majority of situations, but there will be times when you'll have to improvise by combining several retrieves. After letting your lure helicopter down a flooded tree, for instance, you may want to slow-roll it over an adjacent brush pile. Or, you may want to bulge the bait across a weed flat, bump it against an isolated stump on the flat and then helicopter it down a break at the edge of the weeds.

The speed of your retrieve can make a big difference. In most cases, you'll want to reel just fast enough to keep the blades turning, but there will be times when "burning" the bait works much better.

Sometimes spinnerbait strikes are aggressive, but other times, all you'll feel is a slight hesitation in the beat of the blade. Whenever you feel anything out of the ordinary, set the hook.

Always tie your spinnerbait directly to your line, unless you're fishing for pike or muskies. Then, you'll need a braided-wire leader. Many spinnerbaits have an open eye that will not accommodate a snap or swivel. Even if they would, the extra hardware increases the chances of the lure fouling when you cast.

Helicopter a spinnerbait by casting it to vertical cover, such as a rock cliff, flooded tree or breakwall, and then feeding line as the lure slowly sinks with the blade spinning. Keep enough tension on your line so you can feel a pick-up, but not so much that you pull the lure away from the cover.

Recommended Tackle

A 6- to 6¹/₂-foot medium-power baitcasting outfit is adequate for the majority of spinnerbait fishing. The reel should be spooled with 14- to 20-pound-test mono. For big pike or muskies, use a 7¹/₂-foot bucktail rod (p. 52) and a sturdy baitcaster filled with 30- to 50-pound-test Dacron or superline. For crappies and sunfish, use a light- to medium-power spinning outfit with 4- to 6-pound-test mono.

Popular Spinnerbait Retrieves

Slow-roll a spinnerbait over brushy cover, reeling just fast enough to make the blades turn. Allow the blades to bump the brush. Slow-rolling also works well for fishing distinct structure such as a rocky hump, or for crawling over a flat bottom.

A stop-and-go retrieve will usually draw more strikes than a steady retrieve. When you stop reeling, the blade beat changes and the lure flutters downward like an injured bait-fish. Some days, long pauses work best; other days, the fish prefer just a short hesi-tation. You'll have to experiment to find the right tempo.

Bulge the surface with a spinnerbait in the same manner as you would a bucktail. With a spin-nerbait, however, you may want to reel fast enough to make the blades break the surface.

Try reeling a little faster so the blades break the surface. At times, the fish prefer this to a bulging retrieve (left).

Bump your spinnerbait into a stump, stick-up or other type of cover to interrupt the blade's beat and make the lure hesitate. This erratic presentation will draw far more strikes than a steady retrieve.

Tune a spinnerbait by bending the upper shaft so it is perfectly aligned with the lower. If the shaft is canted, the lure will tip to one side.

Add a "stinger hook" to a soft-plastic trailer by threading a long-shank hook into a grub, as shown. Then, push the main hook through the grub and the eye of the stinger.

Shorten the upper arm of a spinnerbait to make it helicopter better. First, cut off a portion of the arm (left) so the blade, when reattached, will ride in front of the hook point. Then, reattach the blade by using needlenose pliers to make a new loop at the end of the arm, as shown (right).

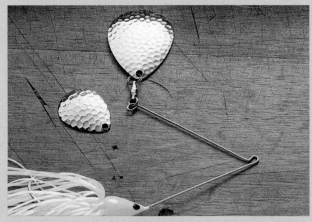

To make a spinnerbait helicopter more slowly, replace the Colorado blade with one a size or two larger. Or, if the lure has an Indiana or willow-leaf blade, replace it with a Colorado.

Tip a spinnerbait with a piece of crawler or other live bait for extra attraction. Use a sidearm lobcast to prevent the bait from tearing off.

Add weight to the hook of your spinnerbait to make the lure run deeper. You can wrap thin-diameter solder around the hook (top) or pinch a sinker onto the hook (bottom).

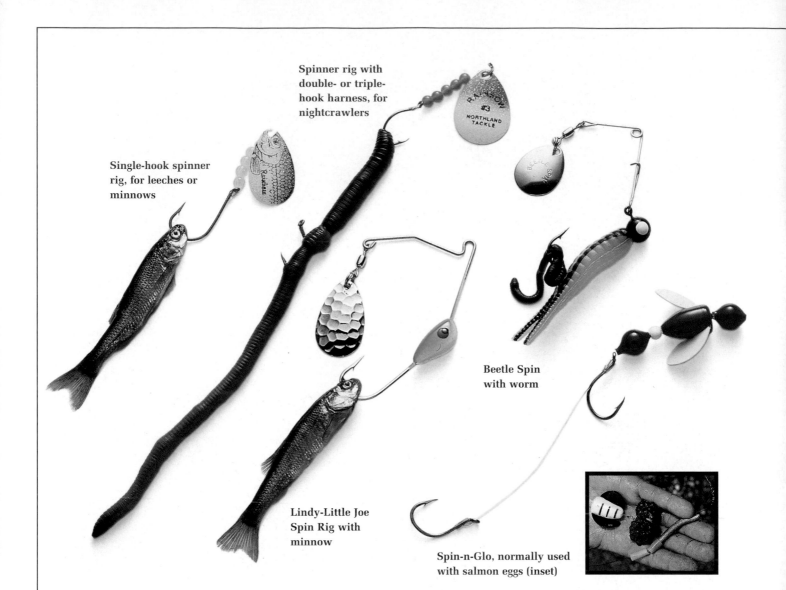

Single-hook spinner rig, for leeches or minnows

Spinner rig with double- or triple-hook harness, for nightcrawlers

Lindy-Little Joe Spin Rig with minnow

Beetle Spin with worm

Spin-n-Glo, normally used with salmon eggs (inset)

SPINNER/ LIVE-BAIT RIGS

Experienced anglers know there are times when a spinner/live-bait combination is far more effective than a spinner or live bait alone.

In discolored water, for example, the vibration of a spinner gets the fishes' attention, drawing them close enough to spot the bait.

A flashing spinner blade also seems to help when fish are "turned off" because of a cold front or some other unfavorable weather condition.

Yet another good time for a spinner/live-bait combo is during a baitfish glut. When food is super-abundant, game-fish may feed for only a few minutes a day and then rest in cover the remainder of the time. They'll often ignore live bait dangled right in their faces, but the flash of a spinner blade may trigger a reaction strike.

Live bait is sometimes fished on a spin-rig or a jig with a safety-pin spinner to work weedy cover. Without the spinner arm to protect the hook, fouling would be a constant problem.

You can buy a variety of spinner rigs designed to be tipped with live bait, but many anglers opt to make their own simply by threading a spinner, clevis and a few beads onto their line in front of the hook. Or, they just tip a weight-forward spinner or a spinnerbait with live bait

Spinner/live-bait combos are commonly used for walleyes, smallmouth bass, northern pike, muskies, crappies, sunfish, trout and salmon. Of course, the type of tackle used with spinner/live-bait rigs depends on the size of the fish and the type of cover you're fishing.

For working deep water, spinner/live-bait combos are usually rigged on a bottom-bouncer or a 3-way-swivel rig.

Spinner Rigs for Heavy Cover

Hook your bait on a jig head and then clip on a safety pin spinner to protect the hook.

Hook your bait on a spin-rig, which is a small, skirtless spinnerbait.

Spinner/Live-Bait Tips

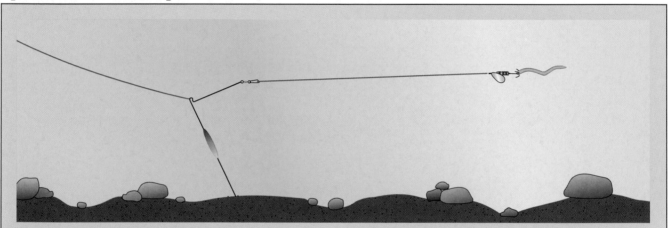

Fish a spinner/live-bait combo on a bottom-bouncer rig. A bottom-bouncer is relatively snag-free and it keeps your spinner riding above snaggy cover.

Use a spinner rig with a quick-change plastic clevis; this way you can switch to a different blade without tying on a whole new rig.

Add a "flicker" blade to your live-bait rig for extra attraction. Just thread on a clevis with a size 0 or 1 Colorado blade (convex side forward), thread on some beads and tie on a bait hook.

SOFT PLASTICS

Manufacturers just keep coming up with improvements on these incredibly lifelike baits.

SOFT PLASTICS

Soft-plastic lures have a big advantage over other types of artificials: not only do they look like real food, they feel like real food.

Rubber baits have been around since the 1860s, but soft plastics (made of polyvinyl chloride resin) are a fairly recent phenomenon. Although the first soft plastics were introduced in 1949, the lures didn't gain widespread popularity until the 1960s.

The first soft-plastic baits available were shaped like a worm, and worms still dominate the soft-plastics market. But today, soft plastics are available in shapes that mimic nearly every conceivable item in a fish's diet.

Many soft-plastic lures are amazingly realistic. They have antennae, fins, legs with realistic toes and other features that give them a natural look. Some soft plastics, such

as "French-fry baits," bear no resemblance to any food item, but are no less effective.

Soft plastics come in a wide range of hardnesses. Some have an extremely soft, almost jellylike texture, which gives them a lively action in the water. But these lures won't last long; after catching a fish or two, they'll be ripped to shreds. Cheap soft plastics are often made of a firm material that has practically no action. The best advice is to buy lures of intermediate hardness.

One big advantage to soft-plastic lures is that they can be rigged "Texas-style," with the hook point buried in the plastic. This way, the lure can be drawn through the heaviest cover without hanging up. A firm hookset will force the point through the plastic and into the fish's jaw.

Another advantage: the soft-plastic material absorbs scent, so any fish attractant that you apply will last a long time. Some soft plastics are impregnated with scent which, according to many experts, makes the fish hold onto the bait a little longer and increases your hooking percentage.

Plastic worm

Lizard

Crayfish

Grub

Slug

Insect

Tube

Salmon eggs

PLASTIC WORMS

Ask a professional bass angler to name his favorite lure, and there's a good chance he'll pick the plastic worm. But worms are not just bass baits; they're used for everything from sunfish to salmon.

Worms used for panfish measure only 2 to 3 inches in length, while those used for Florida largemouths may exceed 14 inches. The majority of largemouth anglers use worms in the 6- to 8-inch range.

Although some worms come pre-rigged, most come without hooks so you'll have to rig them yourself. There are many styles of hooks (opposite) and many different rigging methods (p. 72); versatile anglers are familiar with all of these methods and know when to use each of them.

A Texas-rigged plastic worm is probably the most weedless of all artificial

Curlytail

Augertail

Straight tail

Paddletail

Recommended Tackle

For most worm fishing, you'll need a medium-heavy-power, fast-action baitcasting outfit from 6- to 6 1/2 feet long with 12- to 20-pound mono. A fairly stiff rod is a must for driving the hook through the plastic. A 6-foot, medium-power spinning outfit with 6- to 8-pound-test mono is adequate for fishing small worms (up to 4 inches in length).

lures. You can toss a worm into the densest weed bed and snake it through the cover without picking up a sprig of vegetation. About the only thing that can foul the bait are strands of moss.

The main drawback to a Texas-rigged worm is that the weight carries it to the bottom where weeds or other cover may prevent fish from seeing it. In this situation, try a Carolina rig. Because the bait is separated from the weight, it floats up high enough for fish to get a good look at it.

Plastic worms are known as top baits for weedy cover, but they also work well on a clean bottom. You can work them along the outside of a weedline or over a rock pile or other distinct structure. They are not a good choice for exploring new water, because they must be retrieved slowly.

Many anglers locate fish with a "fast" lure, like a crankbait or spinnerbait, then switch to a worm for more thorough coverage.

Because plastic worms are retrieved so slowly, they're effective in cool water as well as warm. But at water temperatures below 50°F, you may have to downsize your lure. Smaller worms are also a good choice in very clear water. Where the water is muddy, bigger worms, especially those with some type of curly tail, work better.

The main consideration in choosing worms is the type of tail (opposite). Many worms come with some type of curly tail or paddle tail to provide more action, although straight-tail worms are still big sellers.

The worm's hardness is also important. A soft-bodied worm is a good choice for Texas rigging, because the hook point can easily penetrate the plastic on the hookset. And a soft-bodied worm has a lot more tail movement. But a harder body is preferable on pre-rigged worms; otherwise, the hooks would tear out too easily.

Buoyancy makes a difference, as well. Most worms are somewhat buoyant; this way, they ride a little off the bottom where fish can see them. But if a worm is not buoyant enough, it will sink rapidly when you add a worm hook. For surface presentations, you'll need a highly buoyant worm with air bubbles impregnated into the material.

Specialty Worms

Weinee Worm

French Fry

Ringworm

Pre-rigged with plastic legs over hooks

Pre-rigged

Reaper

Worm Hooks

Mister Twister Keeper Hook

Tru-Turn EZ Link

Shaw Grigsby HP Hook

Blue Fox Hidden Head Worm Hook

Tru-Turn Cam Action

Straight Worm Hook

Bent-back Shank Hook

Offset Hook

Worm Hook Tips

Once you've selected a hook style, consider hook size. For a 4-inch worm, use a #1 or 1/0 hook; a 6-inch worm, a 2/0 or 3/0 hook; an 8-inch worm, a 4/0 or 5/0 hook; a 10-inch worm, a 5/0 or 6/0 hook. If your hook doesn't sport barbs or keepers and the worm slides down the shaft, push the worm's head over the hook's eye and anchor it in place with a toothpick (trim off the ends) through the worm and the eye. And keep a file on hand to keep your worm hooks sharp; this will improve your hook-up percentage.

Popular Plastic Worms

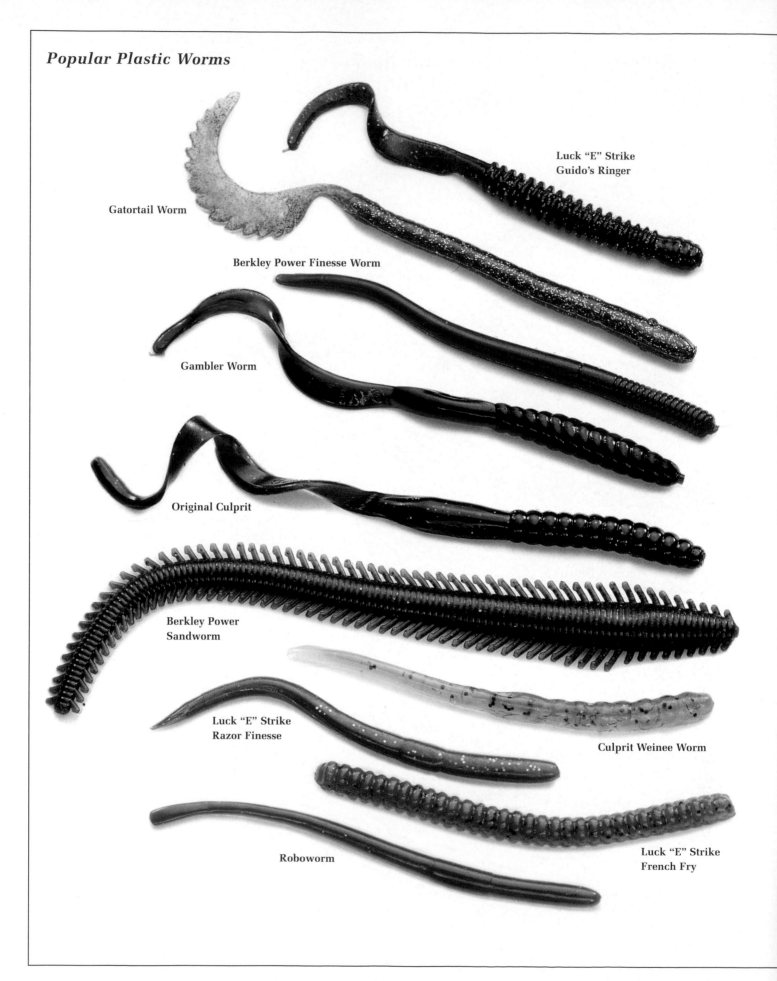

Gatortail Worm

Luck "E" Strike
Guido's Ringer

Berkley Power Finesse Worm

Gambler Worm

Original Culprit

Berkley Power
Sandworm

Luck "E" Strike
Razor Finesse

Culprit Weinee Worm

Roboworm

Luck "E" Strike
French Fry

Artificial Lures

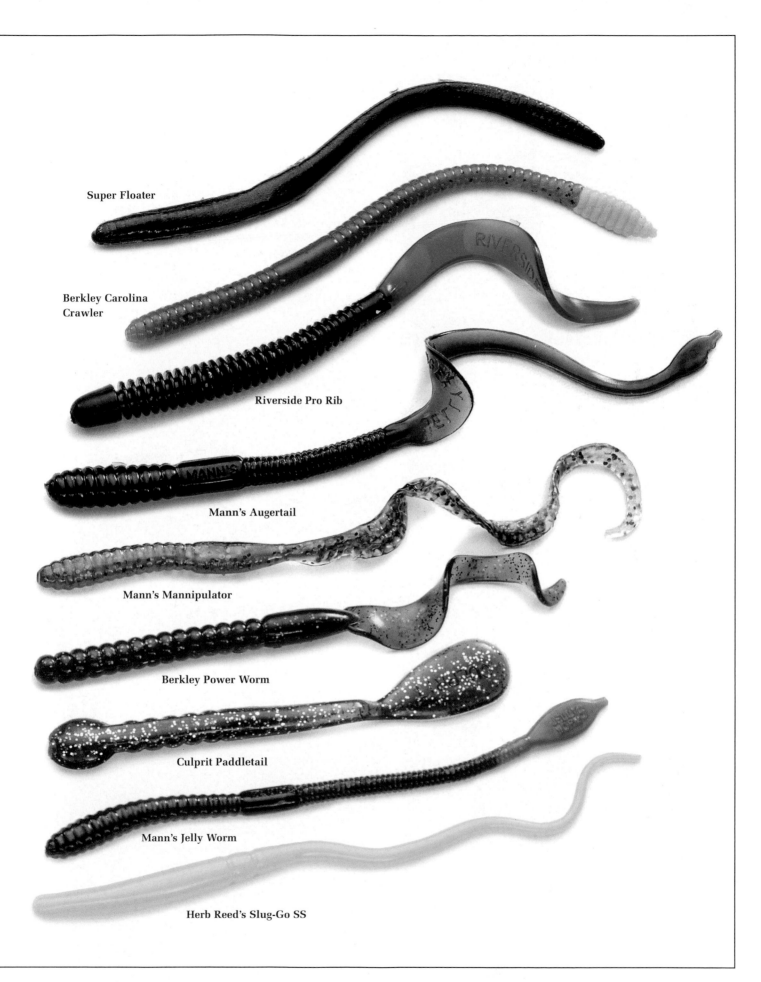

Super Floater

Berkley Carolina Crawler

Riverside Pro Rib

Mann's Augertail

Mann's Mannipulator

Berkley Power Worm

Culprit Paddletail

Mann's Jelly Worm

Herb Reed's Slug-Go SS

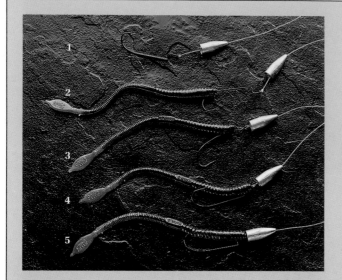

Texas-Rig. *(1) Thread a bullet sinker onto your line and tie on a worm hook. (2) Insert the point of the hook into the head, push it in about $1/2$ inch and bring it out the side. (3) Push the hook all the way through the worm so only the hook eye protrudes at the head. (4) Rotate the hook 180 degrees. (5) Push the hook into the worm; the hook point should almost come out the other side and the worm should hang straight.*

Carolina Rig. *Thread a $1/4$- to 1-ounce bullet sinker and a glass or plastic bead onto your line and attach a barrel swivel. Tie on an 18- to 36-inch leader of lighter mono and attach a worm hook. Push the hook into a buoyant worm and out the side, leaving the point exposed.*

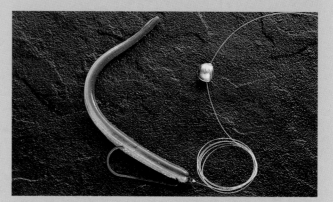

Split-Shot Rig. *Tie a size 1 or 2 worm hook onto 6- or 8-pound mono, add a split shot 12 to 18 inches up the line and Texas-rig a 4-inch worm. This rig is ideal for "finesse" fishing, retrieving very slowly with light line to tempt finicky biters.*

Florida Rig. *Thread a screw-in weight (inset) onto your line and attach a worm hook. Then screw the sinker into the head of the worm. This way, the weight won't separate from the worm when you hang up on a branch or other obstacle.*

Jig Worm. *Attach a mushroom jig to your line and thread on the worm, leaving the hook point exposed. Be sure the worm is snugged up against the flattened head, so there is no gap to catch weeds or debris.*

Fishing a Texas-Rigged Worm

1 *Make a cast and then hold the rod tip at 1 or 2 o'clock as the bait starts to sink. Keep your line slightly taut, but not tight. The fish often grab the worm when it's sinking and if your line is not taut, you won't feel the take.*

2 *Gradually lower your rod tip, keeping your line slightly taut as the bait continues to sink. By the time the bait hits bottom, your rod tip should be at the 3 o'clock position. If you kept your rod tip high, it would be hard to set the hook.*

3 *Continue retrieving with a lift-and-drop motion. When you feel a take or your line starts moving off to the side, drop your rod tip to reduce the tension. If the fish feels too much resistance, it will drop the lure.*

4 *Set the hook with a powerful upward snap of your wrists and forearms. A strong hookset is necessary to drive the hook through the worm and into the fish's jaw.*

Fishing a Carolina-Rigged Worm

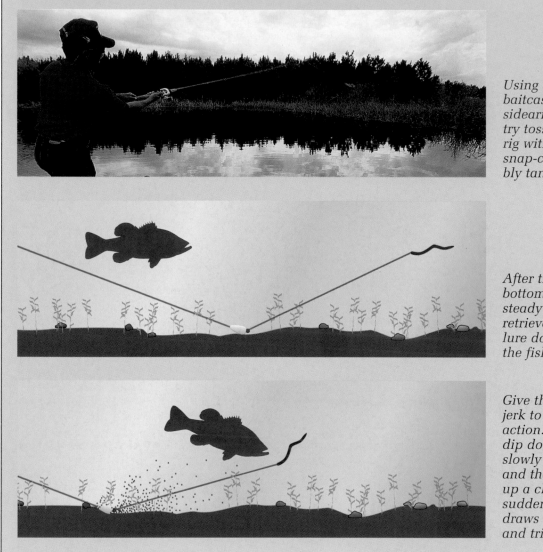

Using a long-handled baitcasting rod, make a sidearm lob-cast. If you try tossing a Carolina rig with an overhand snap-cast, it will probably tangle.

After the sinker hits bottom, begin a slow, steady retrieve. A rapid retrieve will pull the lure down so far that the fish may not see it.

Give the rig a periodic jerk to change the action. The worm will dip down and then slowly float back up, and the sinker will kick up a cloud of silt. The sudden change often draws a fish's attention and triggers a strike.

Other Worm Retrieves

Cast a jig worm along a weedline or into sparse weeds and retrieve slowly. When the open hook hangs up in the vegetation, free it with a sharp jerk of your rod; the bait will jet upward and then flutter back down, drawing a fish's attention.

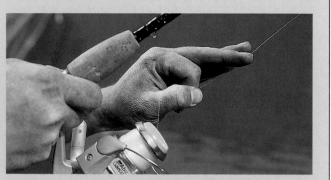

Retrieve a split-shot rig very slowly through cover that you suspect holds fish. A slow retrieve, using your fingers to "stitch" in line, is essential to keep the bait off the bottom. Split-shotting is not a good way to cover lots of water.

Four Tips for Using Plastic Worms

Thread on a brass sinker and a glass bead before tying on your worm hook. The sound of glass clinking against brass makes a sharp sound that the fish can easily detect.

Skip a thick-bodied worm under a dock or other overhead cover by making a sidearm cast with a spinning outfit. Slim-bodied worms do not have enough surface area to skip well.

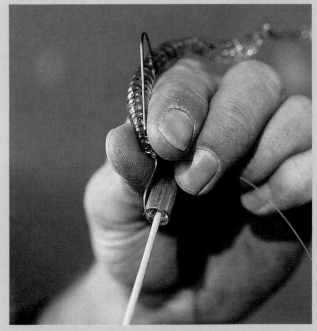

Peg the bullet sinker onto the line so it won't separate from the worm in heavy cover. Just wedge a toothpick into the hole in the sinker and then break off the end.

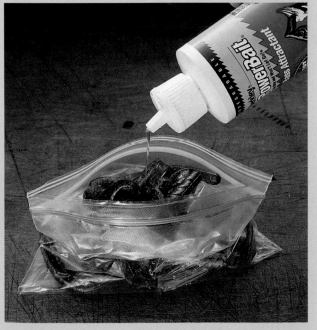

Place your plastic worms in a resealable plastic bag and then add a few drops of worm oil. The oil keeps the worms soft and pliable. Do not mix colors or they will bleed together.

LIZARDS & CRAWS

Some bass anglers swear that a soft-plastic lizard is the most effective bait during the spawning period, because bass will instinctively grab it to prevent it from robbing the nest.

In truth, bass never encounter a live lizard in the water, but they are exposed to salamanders, such as waterdogs and mudpuppies, which look much like soft-plastic lizards.

Numerous food-habit studies have shown that crayfish are a favorite food of smallmouth, largemouth and spotted bass, so it's not surprising that soft-plastic craws work so well for these species.

Craws and lizards can be used interchangeably with plastic worms, but savvy anglers know that there are times when lizards and craws work better. The reason for their effectiveness has less to do with their natural look than the fact that their wiggling arms and pincers make them sink more slowly and

Four Tips for Fishing with Craws & Lizards

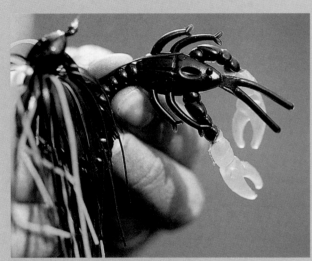

Tip a rubber-legged jig with a soft-plastic craw by threading it onto the hook, as shown. If desired, you can shorten the craw by biting a little off the end before threading it on.

When Texas-rigging a craw or lizard, skin hook the bait by inserting the hook point in the edge rather than the center. Then, when you set the hook, it does not have to penetrate the thick plastic.

Make a "firetail" lizard by dipping the tail in a dye intended for soft plastics. Popular tail colors include chartreuse, hot orange and blue.

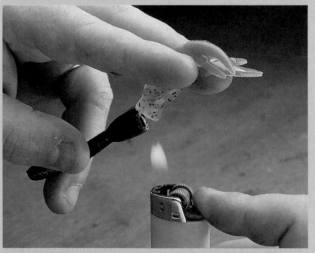

Repair a damaged leg, tail or pincer by melting the plastic with a lighter and pressing the sections together. You can also use this method to splice on a different color tail.

wiggle more enticingly than a worm.

Lizards and craws are most commonly fished on Texas or Carolina rigs (p. 72). Be sure to hook a craw through the narrow end; this way, it will scoot backwards when you retrieve, just like a real crawfish.

You can retrieve lizards and craws in much the same way as you would retrieve a worm, and fish them with the same kind of tackle (p. 68).

Craws, and occasionally small lizards, can also be used as trailers for tipping jigs. Many anglers prefer them over a pork trailer.

Popular Lizards & Craws

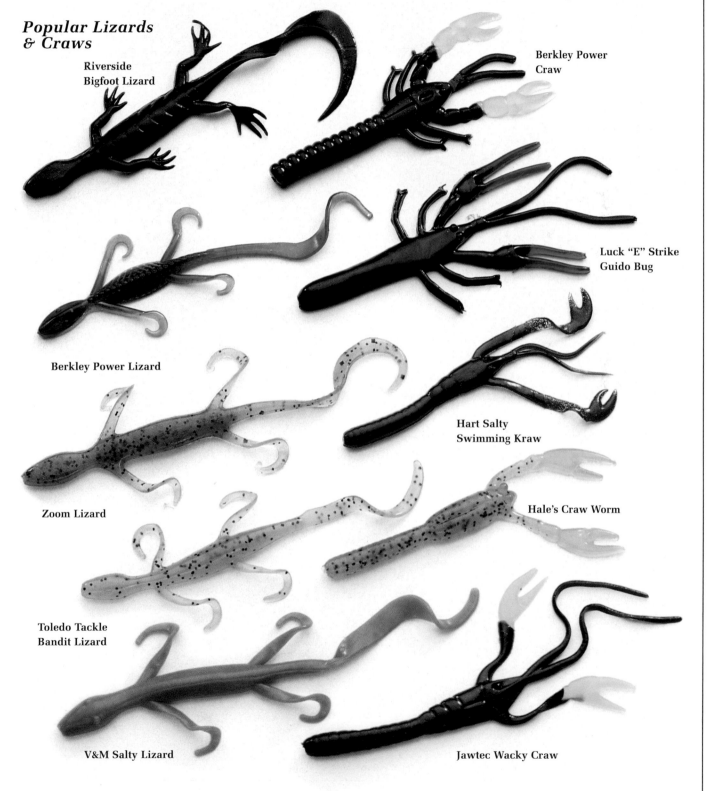

Riverside Bigfoot Lizard

Berkley Power Craw

Luck "E" Strike Guido Bug

Berkley Power Lizard

Hart Salty Swimming Kraw

Zoom Lizard

Hale's Craw Worm

Toledo Tackle Bandit Lizard

V&M Salty Lizard

Jawtec Wacky Craw

GRUBS & TUBEBAITS

The wiggling tail of a soft-plastic grub or the quivering tentacles of a tubebait appeal to all types of gamefish. Grubs and tubebaits from 1 to 2 inches long are deadly for sunfish, crappies, perch, white bass and stream trout; 3- to 5-inchers for bass, walleyes and lake trout; and 6- to 10-inchers for stripers, northern pike and muskies.

Soft-plastic grubs and tube-baits are commonly used as dressings for jigs or trailers for spinnerbaits and other lures, but some types can be fished on their own, much like a plastic worm.

By far the most popular type of grub is the curlytail (sometimes called the twister-tail or screw-tail). The flexible

Basic Types of Grubs & Tubes

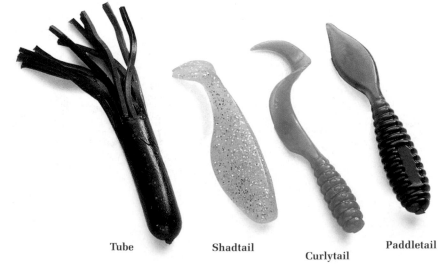

Tube   Shadtail   Curlytail   Paddletail

tail has a built-in curl that creates an irresistible rippling action. Curlytails can be fished on a jig, Texas rig, Carolina rig or split-shot rig.

The second most popular style, the shad-tail, has an expanded end that catches water and gives the tail a lifelike wiggle. It is most commonly fished on a jig.

Both curly-tails and shad-tails work well in dingy water, because the tail creates so much vibration. And they're ideal for fishing in current, because the moving water gives the tail action even when the bait is at rest.

Paddle-tails (also called spear-tails) have a flattened tail that results in a more subtle swimming action. Paddle-tails, which are an excellent choice for rapid retrieves, are usually fished on a jig. They are most popular in saltwater fishing although they are often used in fresh water, as well.

Tubebaits have a hollow body with 20 to 40 tentacles at the rear end. They work best in clear water and rank among the top "sight-fishing" baits. They can be fished on a jig head or rigged on a specially-designed clip-on hook.

Popular Grubs & Tubebaits

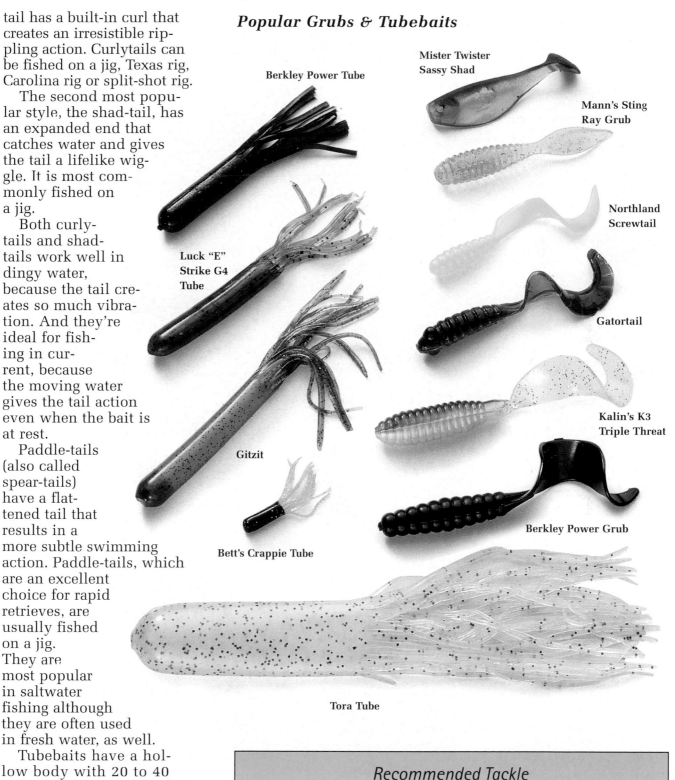

Berkley Power Tube

Mister Twister Sassy Shad

Mann's Sting Ray Grub

Luck "E" Strike G4 Tube

Northland Screwtail

Gitzit

Gatortail

Kalin's K3 Triple Threat

Bett's Crappie Tube

Berkley Power Grub

Tora Tube

Recommended Tackle

When using small- to medium-size grubs and tubes in snag-free water, you can get by with a medium-power spinning outfit and 4- to 8-pound mono. But when using magnum grubs or tubes, or fishing in snaggy cover, use a flippin' stick and mono of at least 15-pound test.

How to Rig Grubs

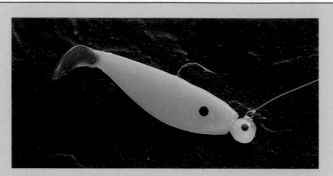

To rig a shad-tail on a jig head, push the hook through the body and out the back, as shown. Make sure the hook comes out the middle of the back.

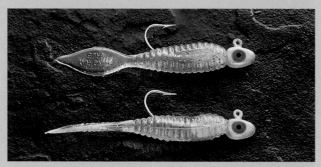

Rig a curlytail grub **(1)** Texas-style with an ordinary bullet sinker, **(2)** Texas-style with "brass 'n' glass," **(3)** Carolina-style with an open hook, **(4)** on a split-shot rig or **(5)** on a jig head by pushing the hook through the body and out the side so the tail rides straight down or straight up.

For the majority of fishing, rig a paddle-tail grub so the tail rides straight up (top). But to slow the sink rate or make the lure skip better, rig the tail so it rides horizontally (bottom).

Two Tips for Fishing with Grubs

Thread on a grub so your hook penetrates the top part of the plastic. This widens your hook gap and improves your hooking percentage.

Make a cavity in a grub body using a razor blade or specially designed tool called a "Grub-Gutter." Then, you can easily insert a float or rattle.

Three Ways to Rig Tubebaits

Thread on a bullet sinker and tie on an Eagle Claw HP hook. Push the hook through the nose of the bait and out the side (left). Push the hook through the tube so the point just barely starts to penetrate the opposite side (middle). Give the hook a half turn, push it through until only the eye protrudes, and then attach the wire clip to the shank (right).

To rig a tube with an internal weight instead of a bullet sinker, drop a specially designed weight down the inside of the tube so the ring rests at the head of the bait (left). Next, push the hook point into the head of the bait and through the ring (right). Then, continue rigging as in the sequence above.

Rig a tube on a jig head by inserting the head into the tube and then pushing on the plastic until the attachment eye pokes through.

Two Tips for Fishing Tubebaits

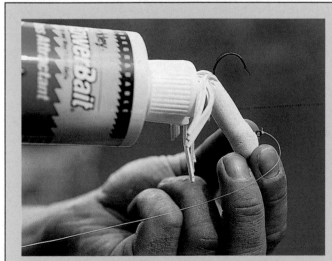

When jigging for lake trout, poke a strip of cut bait into a tube to add scent. A strip from an oily fish, like a smelt or herring, works best. Or, push some cotton into the tube and soak it with bottled scent.

Jiggle a tubebait in front of an inactive bass to tempt a strike. Try to make the tentacles dance enticingly without moving the bait away from the fish.

SOFT JERKBAITS

Soft jerkbaits are one of the few really "new" lure innovations in recent years. When fished with an erratic twitch-and-pause retrieve, these slow-sinking baits will draw strikes from the fussiest bass.

Bass anglers rely mainly on the 6-inch baits, but when fishing gets especially tough,

dropping down to the 3-inch size may draw strikes.

But soft jerkbaits, also called jerkworms, soft stick-baits or slugs, are not just bass lures. Larger jerkbaits (up to 10 inches in length) work well for stripers, muskies and pike, and anglers in the northern Canada have found them to be a great bait for giant lakers.

What makes soft jerkbaits different than other soft plastics is their slow sink rate, which gives them a unique, wounded-baitfish action. They dart upward a little and then slowly settle back down.

A soft jerkbait looks a lot like a plastic worm, but it is designed to ride horizontally in the water, not sink nose-down, like a worm. You can fish a soft jerkbait on the surface in walk-the-dog fashion (p. 36), or let it sink a foot or two before starting your retrieve.

Soft jerkbaits are at their best in spring, when bass are in a negative mood following spawning. But the lures will work any time the fish are in shallow water. They are not particularly good deep-water baits; weighting them to sink defeats the purpose, although they can be fished on a Carolina rig. They produce little vibration, so they do not work well in muddy water.

Soft jerkbaits are hard to fish in windy weather, because the wind puts a bow in your line and pulls the bait along too fast.

Popular Soft Jerkbaits

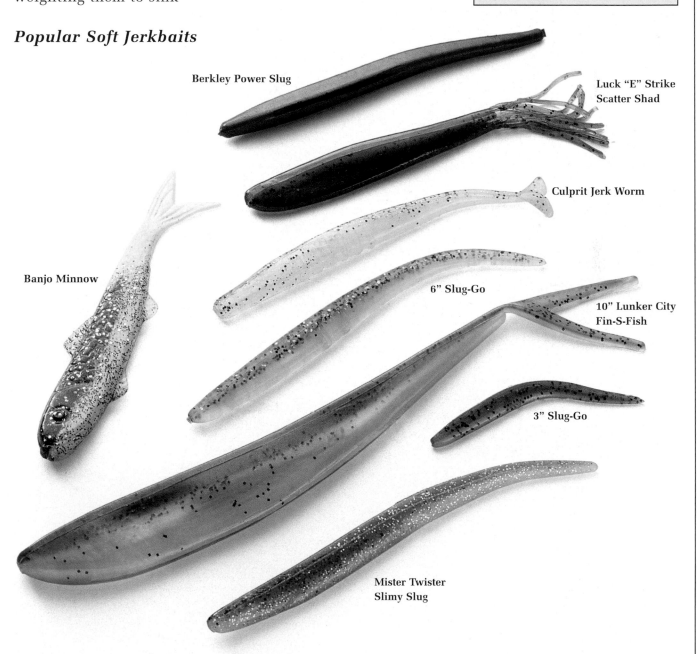

Berkley Power Slug

Luck "E" Strike Scatter Shad

Culprit Jerk Worm

Banjo Minnow

6" Slug-Go

10" Lunker City Fin-S-Fish

3" Slug-Go

Mister Twister Slimy Slug

How to Rig a Soft Jerkbait

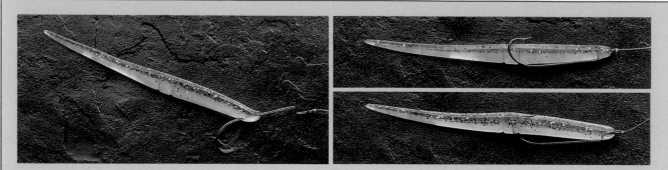

Push an offset worm hook into a soft jerkbait as far as the offset (left), then bring the hook out the bottom, turn it 180 degrees (top right) and push it through the body so the point rests in the depression on the back (bottom right).

How to Fish a Soft Jerkbait

Wind

1 Cast with the wind to reduce backlashing and prevent the wind from putting a bow in your line and pulling the bait too fast.

2 With your rod tip angled downward, give the lure a gentle pull, not a sharp jerk.

3 Pause while the bait glides upward and to the side and slowly sinks back down, then give the bait another gentle pull. It should glide to the other side.

4 When you feel a fish grab the bait and start swimming away with it, set the hook with a sideways sweep of the rod.

Four Tips for Fishing with Jerkbaits

To make the bait run deeper, push a lead insert or finishing nail into the plastic just ahead of the hook bend. An insert will also give you longer casts and keep the wind from blowing the bait too fast.

Don't attempt to fish with a soft jerkbait that is warped from being stored with a bend. It will not have the desired side-to-side action. Boil the bait later to remove the bend (see below).

Boil a warped bait to remove the bend. Check the bait after about 30 seconds; boiling it too long will soften it too much. Then, lay the bait on its back, making sure it is perfectly straight.

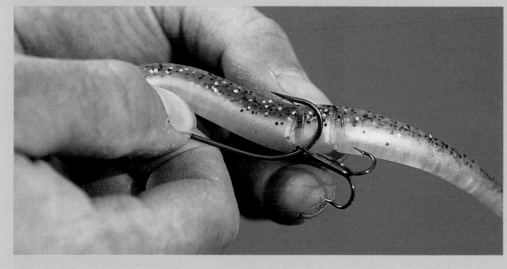

Add a stinger hook to improve your hooking percentage in snag-free cover. Just slip a size 4 treble over the worm hook before pushing it into the bait.

SOFT-PLASTIC SPECIALTY BAITS

If you flip through the pages of your favorite fishing-tackle catalog, you'll see an astonishing variety of soft-plastic baits ranging in size from tiny imitation salmon eggs to "snakes" a foot and a half long.

Most soft-plastic specialty baits look like real food, but some bear no resemblance to a natural food item. Instead, they rely on impregnated scent to attract fish.

Although soft plastics can't duplicate the natural wiggle of live bait squirming on the hook, they have some major advantages over the real thing: they're a lot more durable, and you don't have to drive miles out of your way to find a bait shop.

Plastic salmon eggs are a godsend to trout and salmon anglers. Fresh eggs are available only seasonally, and even when you can get them, it's difficult to keep them fresh and make them stay on the hook. Some imitation eggs have an extremely soft texture, like that of a real egg, so when fish grab them, they don't let go. Many fake eggs have egg scent molded into them.

You can buy soft-plastic imitations of a variety of adult insects, including grasshoppers, crickets, spiders, ants and even flies. Larval-insect imitations, such as hellgrammites and mayfly wigglers, are also available. Insect baits are most commonly used for panfish and stream trout.

Although many anglers rely on the soft-plastic craws mentioned earlier in the chapter, these bait are not

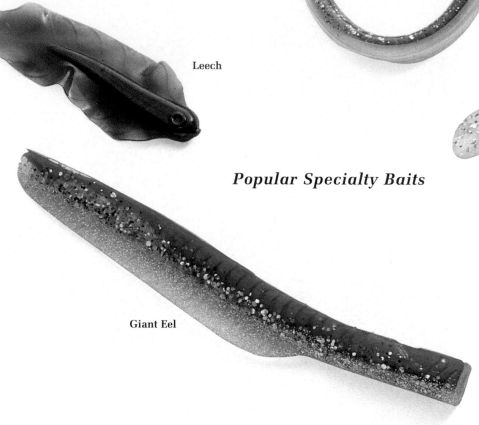

Popular Specialty Baits

Leech

Giant Eel

very realistic. Some manufacturers, however, offer imitation crayfish that are made using molds of the real thing. You can also buy ultra-realistic replicas of many other common crustaceans, such as shrimp and scuds. Lifelike crustacean imitations are a favorite of anglers seeking bass and large stream trout.

Giant soft-plastic baits are made to mimic trout, eels, waterdogs, snakes and other large food items. Used mainly for stripers and large Florida bass, these baits are also catching on among pike, muskie and lake trout anglers.

Many of these giant baits are made by local "basement" operators, so they may

be difficult to find. But the market for these baits is growing, and more established manufacturers are adding them to their lines.

Most soft-plastic specialty baits come without hooks, so you'll have to rig them yourself using the techniques shown earlier. But many of the smaller baits, including a number of insect baits, come with hooks molded in.

Opposite: Specialty baits can draw bites when nothing else will work.

Giant Worm

Giant Shad

Cricket

Egg Cluster

Crawfish

Sculpin

How to Rig a Soft-Plastic Salmon Egg

Using a short-shank egg hook, **(1)** skin hook the egg, then **(2)** turn the hook 180 degrees and **(3)** insert the point into the opposite side of the egg.

How to Rig Other Specialty Baits

Rig an egg cluster onto a small treble hook, pushing two of the hooks into the plastic and leaving the third hook exposed.

Thread a worm hook into a soft-plastic crayfish by starting just above the tail and pushing it through until it comes out the snout, point up.

Rig an insect bait by threading it head-first onto a long-shank Aberdeen hook. The hook point should come out the abdomen.

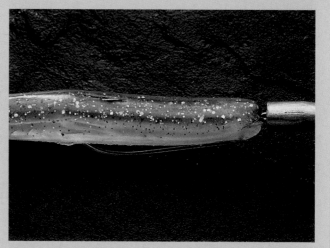

Rig a giant soft-plastic Texas-style or Carolina-style on a size 3/0 to 6/0 worm hook. When Texas-rigging, the point of the hook should penetrate the plastic.

Five Tips for Fishing Soft-Plastic Specialty Baits

Fish a larval-insect imitation behind a plastic casting bubble. The bubble not only provides casting weight, it keeps the bait floating above weedy, brushy or rocky cover.

When Texas-rigging a giant soft-plastic, use a razor blade to cut a groove in the back. This way the hook point can rest in the groove for easier hooking, just as it does on a soft jerkbait (p. 84).

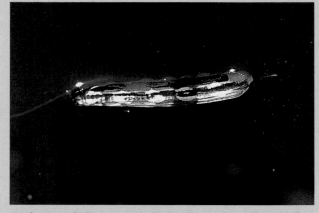

Fish an adult insect imitation, such a dragonfly, on the surface with no weight. This technique works well for bass and sunfish when bugs are hatching on a warm summer evening.

Tip a teardrop or other tiny jig with a soft-plastic grub to catch catch crappies, sunfish, perch and even trout. This rig works well in open water or through the ice.

When river fishing with a single egg imitation or an egg cluster, use a drift-fishing rig. Splice a three-way swivel into your line, tie on a dropper and pinch on a drift sinker. Should the sinker snag, it will easily pull off the line and you can pinch on another.

JIGGING LURES

*W*hen it comes to tempting bites from stubborn gamefish, nothing is as effective as the tantalizing action of a jigging lure.

JIGGING LURES

Anglers equipped with a good selection of jigging lures can catch practically any kind of freshwater game-fish. The major types of jigging lures include:

- **Lead-head jig** – This is nothing more than a chunk of lead with a hook molded into it. Normally, the hook is covered with a hair, feather, tinsel or soft-plastic dressing.
- **Jigging spoon** – A thick metal spoon that sinks rapidly and has an erratic, tumbling action.
- **Vibrating blade** – With its thin metal body and lead head, this lure vibrates rapidly when pulled upward.
- **Tailspinner** – A heavy lead head makes it possible to cast this lure a long distance. The spinner on

the tail turns when the lure is jigged upward and helicopters as it sinks back down.

In addition, anglers can choose from a selection of jigging lures designed primarily for ice fishing. Some of these lures, such as tear drops and swimming minnows (p. 111), are now becoming popular for open-water fishing, as well.

Because jigging lures are relatively heavy for their size, they work better than most other lures in deep water or current.

The fact that fish often strike a jigging lure as it is sinking has some important implications for anglers. For instance, it pays to choose the lightest lure that will still reach the desired depth; this way, the lure has a slow

sink rate, and fish have more time to react to it.

When the lure is sinking, you must keep your line tight enough that you can feel the strike, but not so tight that the lure doesn't sink freely. If you have too much slack in your line, you won't feel the strike at all.

Each type of jigging lure is fished a little differently, as is explained on the pages that follow.

Types of Jigs & Jigging Lures

Lead-head jig **Vibrating blade** **Tailspinner** **Jigging spoon**

A jig and curlytail grub will catch everything from sunfish to walleyes to stripers.

LEAD-HEAD JIGS

Although a jig is among the simplest of fishing lures, jig selection is not so simple. Here are the things you need to consider when buying jig heads and dressings:

Jig Heads

The jig head determines how fast the jig will sink and how well it will hook the fish that strike. It also affects the jig's action. Here are the main things to remember when selecting jig heads:
- **Head Shape** – Standard round jig heads work well for most jig fishing. Because of the way the hook eye is positioned in the head, the jig is well balanced, meaning that it hangs horizontally when tied to the line, so it resembles a swimming minnow. Plus, round-head jigs sink quickly, which is what is needed most of the time.

But there are times when other types of heads work better. In strong current, for instance, a bullet-head jig is hard to beat because it slips easily through the current and stays down better than any other type of head.

A slider-head jig, one with a horizontally flattened body, is the best choice for swimming over weed tops or any shallow-water obstructions. It sinks very slowly and has an attractive gliding action. Some have an upturned nose for even more lift.

Fishing in weeds is a problem with most jig heads, because they have a hook eye that protrudes from the top and catches bits of vegetation. A cone-shaped head with the hook eye right at the front tip slips through the weeds more easily.

A football-head jig has a unique rocking action. When the head wedges against a rock, a pull on the line causes the body to tip up in what has been described as a crayfish taking a defensive posture.

On a stand-up jig, the bottom of the head is flattened, so the jig rests with the hook pointing up. This design is relatively snag-free, and the upright position makes the jig more visible.

Mushroom-head jigs are an excellent choice for rigging with soft plastics, because the trailer abuts snugly with the flattened head, and the double barbs on the collar prevent it from sliding back, even when the bait is ripped through weeds.

Banana-head jigs work well for vertical jigging, because the attachment eye at the front gives the bait an exaggerated kicking action.

Keel jigs work well in deep water or fast current. The head has a vertically flattened shape that slices through the water easily and sinks rapidly.

Artificial Lures

Common Head Styles

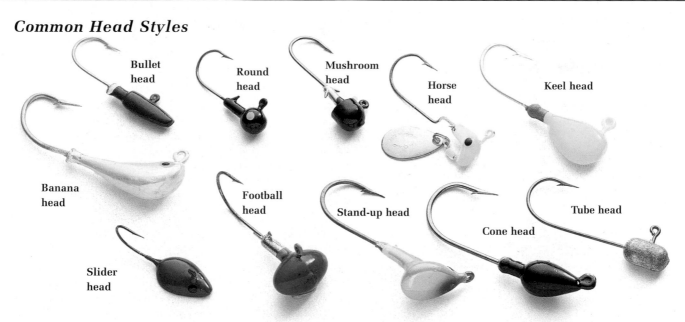

Bullet head

Round head

Mushroom head

Horse head

Keel head

Banana head

Football head

Stand-up head

Tube head

Cone head

Slider head

Horsehead jigs, also called pony jigs, have a horselike snout to which is attached a spinner blade. They are often used for casting or trolling in open water.

Tube heads are designed to fit inside of hollow, soft-plastic tubebaits. Insert the entire head inside the tube and push the attachment eye through the plastic. Rigged this way, the tube is firmly secured to the jig head.

- **Head Weight** – The general rule in choosing a jig head is to use just enough weight so the lure can reach bottom. The lighter the head, the slower the sink rate, so the fish get a better look at it.

  Remember that you'll always need a little more weight to get down when fishing in wind or current. And a bulky trailer will also slow your sink rate, meaning that you'll need more weight.
- **Shank Length** – The best shank length depends on whether or not you're tipping with live bait. A short-shank jig is the best choice for tipping; with the jig head closer to the bait, you get fewer short strikes.

A long-shank hook is a better choice for any kind of jig with a tail. The farther the hook extends back in the tail, the greater your hooking percentage.

- **Shank Diameter** – A thin-wire hook is best when tipping with live bait, because it does less damage to the bait than would a thick hook. And should you get snagged on a log, a strong, steady pull on the line will usually straighten the hook enough to free the jig. The obvious drawback to a thin-wire hook is that you risk losing a big fish. If you're using heavy tackle for big fish, use a hook with a shank thick enough so it won't straighten.
- **Hook Size** – If you're tipping your jig with a minnow, a soft-plastic grub or a pork chunk, you need a hook with enough gap to make the hook protrude well above the dressing. If the gap is too narrow, the point will rest right on the dressing and won't penetrate the fish's mouth.

- **Weedguards** – If you'll be fishing in weedy or woody cover, your hook should have some kind of weedguard or brushguard. Bristle-type weedguards are the most popular, although some anglers prefer the wire or plastic types. The weedguard should be stiff enough to protect the hook, but not so stiff that it significantly lowers your hooking percentage.

Types of Weedguards

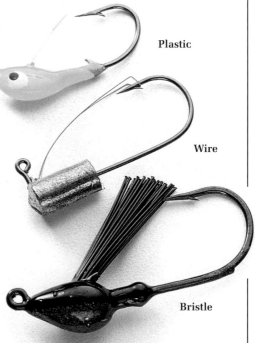

Plastic

Wire

Bristle

Jig Dressings

Some jigs come dressed with hair, feathers or synthetic material, but others must be dressed with a soft-plastic grub, a plastic worm, a pork "product" or live bait.

Types of Jig Dressings

Live rubber

Bucktail

Tinsel

Marabou

Chicken feather

Soft plastic

The dressing gives the jig its action, adds color and helps control the sink rate. A bulky plastic tail, for example, is much more buoyant than a sparse hair or feather tail, making a jig of the same weight sink more slowly.

Soft-plastic dressings have great action, look and feel like real food, and are inexpensive. The best ones are very soft and pliable, and the material is very thin, so the tail wiggles enticingly, even on a very slow retrieve or when held motionless in slow current.

Jigs can be tipped with practically any of the soft plastics shown on pages 67-87. In addition, jigs are commonly dressed with a soft-plastic body with a marabou insert.

Bucktail is one of the oldest jig dressings, but is just as effective today as ever. Because deer hair is hollow, the fibers are highly buoyant. They tend to flare out and have more of a "breathing" action than do synthetic fibers. Bucktail jigs must be well-tied, with a heavy wrapping of thread coated with a layer of epoxy. Otherwise, fibers will start to fall out after a few casts, the wraps will loosen and all the hair will fall off the bait.

Feather jigs, including marabou and chicken-feather models, may be hard to find because they're difficult to tie. But many anglers swear by them; they have a breathing action that is even more intense than that of a bucktail.

If you're tipping your jig with live bait, a tail may not even be necessary; in fact, it may detract from the bait's natural attraction. But if you do use a tail, it should be short and sparse so it doesn't cover up too much of the bait. Good choices include a small tube-bait, a sparsely tied feather jig or a soft-plastic/marabou body.

How to Tip Jigs with Live Bait

Minnow through lips

Minnow through mouth and out top of head

Half a crawler

Leech above sucker

Popular Lead-Head Jigs

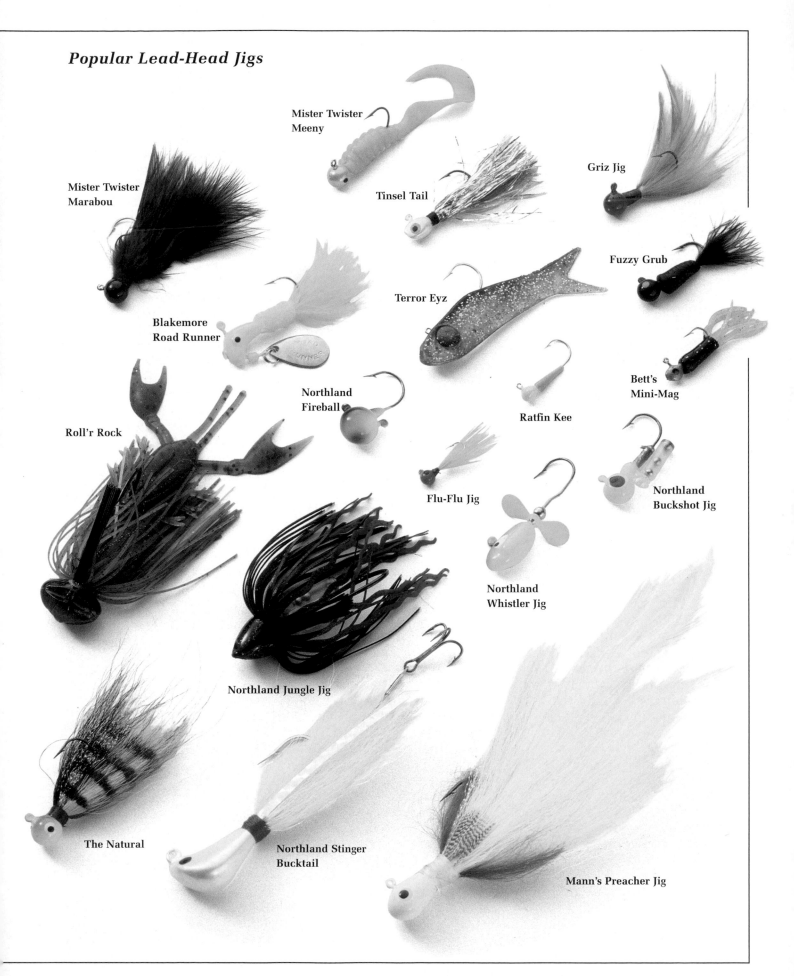

Mister Twister Meeny

Mister Twister Marabou

Tinsel Tail

Griz Jig

Fuzzy Grub

Terror Eyz

Blakemore Road Runner

Bett's Mini-Mag

Roll'r Rock

Northland Fireball

Ratfin Kee

Flu-Flu Jig

Northland Buckshot Jig

Northland Whistler Jig

Northland Jungle Jig

The Natural

Northland Stinger Bucktail

Mann's Preacher Jig

Jig-Fishing Techniques

Ask a dozen anglers to describe the best way to fish a jig and you'll get a dozen different answers. And under the right set of circumstances, all of them could be right.

Among the factors that influence how you fish a jig are: water clarity, water temperature, depth, current speed, weather conditions, time of day and mood of the fish. It's not always possible to predict in advance what type of retrieve will work best; you just have to experiment.

The most popular methods of fishing a jig are described below and on the following pages, but regardless of what technique you use, certain principles always apply:

• Fish tend to hit a jig on the drop, so you should keep a little tension on your line as the jig is sinking; otherwise, you won't feel the take. Don't keep your line too tight, however, or the jig won't have the right action.

• Becoming a proficient jig fisherman requires a delicate "feel" and fast reflexes, so it's important to concentrate. Fish often hit a jig with a solid thump or tap, but that's not always the case. Any twitch, hesitation or sideways movement of the line may signal a take. Or, sometimes the jig just doesn't sink because a fish has grabbed it.

• At the first hint of a strike, set the hook. When a fish takes a jig, it flares its gills and sucks in a volume of water that includes the jig; if you hesitate and the fish feels anything out of the ordinary, it will expel the jig as fast as it sucked it in.

The majority of jig fishermen use one of the following retrieves, or some variation of it:

• **Dragging** – Slowly retrieving the jig with very little, if any, vertical action, works well when the fish are lethargic because of cold water or when they're in a negative feeding mood. Although the jig is usually dragged along bottom or over the weedtops, you can also swim it slowly in midwater to catch suspended fish.

• **Lift-and-Drop** – This common retrieve involves giving the jig a short twitch (usually no more than a few inches long), keeping your line taut as it sinks back to the bottom, and then twitching it again. Experiment with the length of the twitches and the duration of the pauses until you find the tempo that works best on a given day. The twitch-and-pause retrieve can also be used to catch fish suspended far off the bottom.

• **Rip-Jigging** – This technique gives your jig an erratic action that may trigger strikes when other jigging methods fail. Before your jig sinks all the way to the bottom, give it a hard jerk, throw slack into the line on the drop, and then jerk again before the jig touches bottom. Fish usually grab the jig as it is sinking and, when you jerk the next time, the fish is hooked. This retrieve keeps the jig dancing above the fish's head and darting erratically, like an injured baitfish.

Any of these basic retrieves can be used whether you're casting, trolling or vertically jigging (opposite).

Always attach your jig directly to the line; it will not cause line twist (unless you're jigging vertically), so there is no need for a snap-swivel. Nor is there any need for a leader, except when fishing for pike or muskies. Then, a short wire "striker" (p. 100) will suffice.

When tipping jigs with live bait, you're often faced with the decision as to whether or not to use a "stinger" hook (p. 101). A stinger may be a big help when fish are striking short, but it usually reduces the number of strikes you'll get and increases fouling problems. The best strategy is to let the fish tell you when a stinger is needed. If you're missing more fish than you're hooking, add a stinger hook.

Recommended Tackle

The length and power of the rod and the weight of the line depend on what species of fish you're after and what kind of cover you're working.

No matter what type of jig fishing you're doing, sensitivity is a major issue, so you'll want a high-modulus graphite rod with a fast tip. The fast tip not only makes it easier to detect strikes, it gives you a quicker hookset. A slow-action rod takes a fraction of a second longer to transfer the power of the hookset to the jig, giving fish more time to eject it.

Most jig fishermen prefer monofilament line, because its stretch allows fish to easily suck in the jig. Missed strikes are common when jigging with superline, because the lack of stretch prevents fish from taking the jig as deeply.

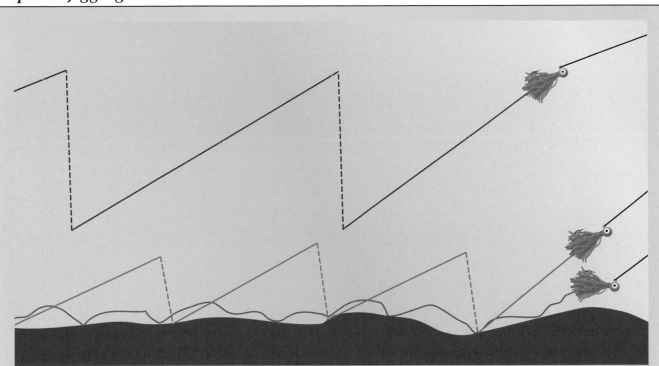

Basic jig retrieves include dragging (blue line), lift-and-drop (green line) and rip-jigging (red line).

Vertical jigging involves lowering your jig to the bottom and hopping it vertically as your boat drifts with the wind or current. For the best feel, use your trolling motor to hold the boat directly over your jig so your line stays as vertical as possible.

Jig trolling is not much different than trolling a crankbait, but you must move slowly enough that your jig can touch bottom. Most anglers backtroll for good boat control while working the jig with the lift-and-drop method.

Tip a jig with a bulky pork or plastic trailer to slow its sink rate and give fish a longer look at the bait. When the fish are fussy, this can make a big difference.

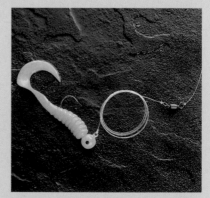

If your bristle weedguard is so stiff that you're missing fish, remove some of the bristles to make it more flexible.

Make a wire striker for pike or muskie fishing by twisting a length of single-strand stainless-steel wire to your jig and a barrel swivel. The striker should be only 4 to 6 inches long.

Splice a small barrel swivel into your line, about 18 inches from your jig, when vertically jigging. Otherwise, your line will twist badly and continually throw loops around your rod tip.

Flatten a ball-head jig to convert it to a slider head. Then, you can work it slowly over weed tops or other obstructions without it constantly snagging.

Attach a small float above your jig when fishing over woody or weedy cover. Give the float a twitch and then hesitate as the jig swings back to vertical; that's when the fish usually strike.

Outfit your jig with a stinger hook by **(1)** clipping a commercially made stinger onto a jig that has a bottom eye, **(2)** pushing a commercially made stinger with a latex-filled loop over the bend of your jig hook or **(3)** making your own stinger by tying a length of stiff mono to the bend of your jig hook and then adding a treble hook.

Do not insert the stinger into the tail of a minnow; it will impede its swimming action and reduce the number of strikes. Instead, let the stinger trail near the minnow's tail.

FLOATERS

This lure category includes floating jigs and floats that are threaded onto your line. These lures are normally used in combination with live bait.

Floaters add a splash of color and lift your bait above weeds and other cover, where fish can see it more easily. They also work well for keeping your bait from constantly fouling on a bottom covered with moss.

Floaters are most popular for walleyes, smallmouth bass, trout and salmon, but can be used for most any gamefish.

Floating jigs resemble ordinary jigs but the head, instead of being made of lead, is made of styrofoam, cork or some other highly buoyant material. Floating jigs are sometimes tipped with a soft-plastic grub instead of live bait.

Floats that thread onto your line come in a variety of shapes, the most common being a simple round ball, or corkie. Some floats have wings that make them spin when retrieved, adding vibration as well as visual appeal. Others are intended to look like a gob of salmon eggs.

You can peg a float with a toothpick to keep it away from the hook, but most anglers just let it slide on the line; the buoyancy keeps it pushed against the hook eye.

Floaters used for trout and salmon are usually fished on a split-shot rig; those used for walleyes and smallmouth bass, on a slip-sinker rig (opposite).

When used with an extremely long leader, floating jigs and other floaters can help you reach suspended fish. But there is a common misconception as to how far they will lift the bait off bottom. Some anglers use leaders as much as 15 feet long under the mistaken assumption that they'll be able to float their bait up to reach fish 10 or more feet off the bottom. But, unless you're using a very large floater or moving extremely slowly, you'll be lucky to raise it more than two or three feet. It's just a matter of physics; there is simply not enough buoyancy to overcome the water resistance.

A light leader is a must when using any type of floater. If your leader is too heavy, the extra water resistance will keep the floater down.

Popular Floaters

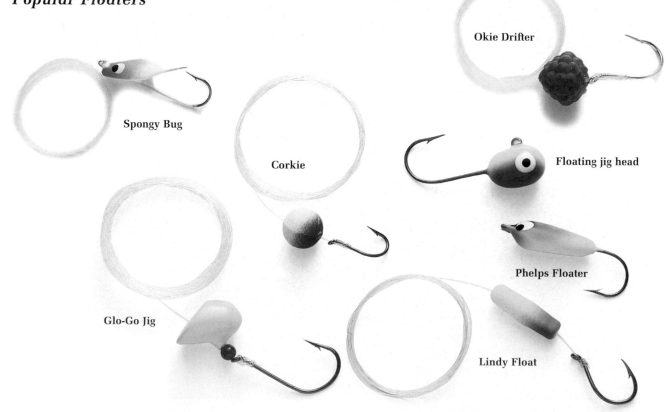

Spongy Bug

Corkie

Okie Drifter

Floating jig head

Glo-Go Jig

Phelps Floater

Lindy Float

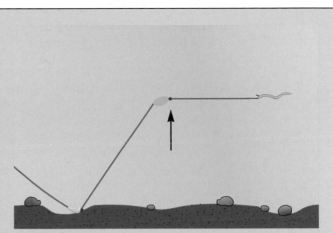

Make an adjustable floating rig by threading a slip-sinker onto your line, adding a neoprene stop and then tying on a floater. When you want the bait to float higher, slide the stop farther from the hook.

Add a second neoprene stop between the float and the hook; this way you can keep the float away from the hook so the bait looks more natural.

Make a drift-fishing rig for trout and salmon by tying on a floater, such as an Okie Drifter (left) tipped with fresh or soft-plastic salmon eggs, and pinching on just enough split shot to keep the rig bumping bottom as it drifts. Angle a short cast upstream and, with your rod tip high, let the rig float through a run.

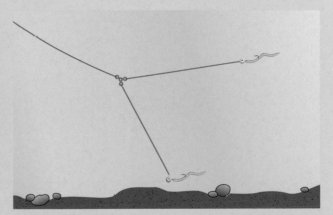

For fishing in low-growing weeds, use a slip-sinker rig made with a bullet sinker and a floater. The sinker slides through the weeds easily and the floater keep the bait riding above the weed tops.

Fish a floating jig tipped with live bait on a 3-way swivel rig, using a lead-head jig for weight. This rig improves your odds, because a fish has the choice of taking the floater or the lead-head.

JIGGING SPOONS

Until recently, the jigging spoon was considered a deep-water bass bait, but anglers are discovering that these simple lures also work well for other gamefish such as lake trout, walleyes and even yellow perch.

A jigging spoon consists of a piece of lead, brass or stainless steel with a hook on the end of it. Most jigging spoons weigh from 1/2 to more than 2 ounces, although some panfish models weigh only 1/8- to 1/4-ounce.

Long, thin spoons sink rapidly and are intended primarily for vertical jigging. Short, wide models (called slab spoons) are designed for distance casting. They make good shad imitations and are ideal for "jump fishing" for white bass and stripers.

To vertically jig a spoon, let it sink to the bottom, lift it from 6 to 18 inches, and then follow it back down with your rod tip until you feel it touch bottom. It's important to maintain contact with the spoon as it is sinking; if you allow the line to go slack, you won't feel the strike.

As in any kind of jig fishing, you must experiment to find the right jigging action. Some days, a big lift followed by a long pause works best; other days, a fast, short jigging stroke is more effective.

A good depth finder is a big help in vertical jigging, because it enables you to see fish that are suspended off the bottom and adjust your presentation accordingly. Reel the lure up and jig it just above the fish.

Because of the open hooks, hang-ups are common when vertically jigging in timber or other heavy cover. But if you get snagged, simply pull the line tight and then let the spoon drop; its heavy weight usually frees the hook.

Recommended Tackle

It's not uncommon to vertically jig in depths of 50 feet or more, so you'll need a long rod to get a solid hookset. Expert spoon jiggers prefer a 6 1/2- to 7-foot, medium-heavy-power graphite baitcasting rod with a long handle and a sturdy baitcasting reel spooled with 20-pound mono. Lighter line would result in too many break-offs.

Spoon Jigging Tips

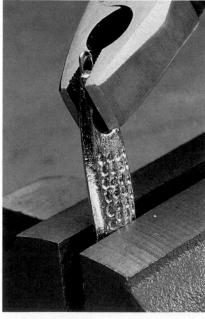

Bend a jigging spoon slightly to change its action. A bent spoon will flutter more erratically as it sinks than a straight one.

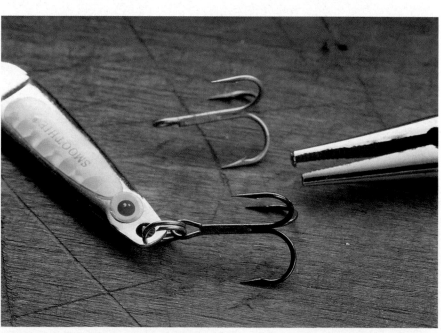

Replace cheap nickel hooks with quality bronze hooks that are sharper and straighten more easily when you get snagged. If the lure does not have a split-ring on the attachment eye, add one to improve the action and prevent damaging your line.

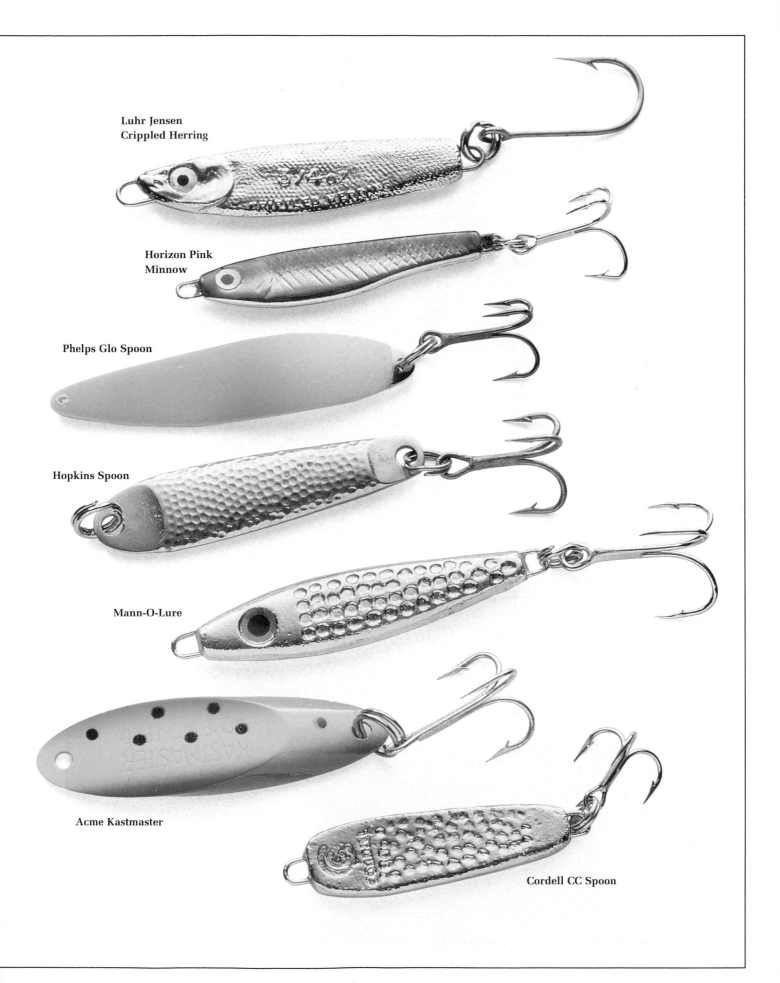

Luhr Jensen
Crippled Herring

Horizon Pink
Minnow

Phelps Glo Spoon

Hopkins Spoon

Mann-O-Lure

Acme Kastmaster

Cordell CC Spoon

VIBRATING BLADES

As their name suggests, vibrating blades have an intense wiggle that attracts gamefish, even in waters where the visibility is only a few inches. Fish detect the strong vibrations using their lateral lines.

A vibrating blade, also called a bladebait, consists of a thin, fish-shaped metal body with lead molded onto the head. The attachment eye is on the back, so the bait vibrates rapidly when pulled upward.

Some bladebaits come with more than one attachment hole along the back. By clipping your snap into different holes, you can change the bait's action. With the snap attached to the front hole, the bait has a very tight wiggle; to the rear hole, a looser wobble.

Small bladebaits, weighing as little as $\frac{1}{8}$ ounce, are commonly used for panfish; medium-size baits ($\frac{1}{4}$ to $\frac{1}{2}$ ounce) for walleyes and black bass; and large baits (up to 1 ounce) for stripers and lake trout.

Although bladebaits are used mainly for vertical jigging, they can also be reeled steadily, like a crankbait, or fished with a twitch-and-pause retrieve, like a lead-head jig.

Vertical jigging with a bladebait is not much different than vertical jigging with a lead-head jig. But blades are often fished with a much longer vertical sweep, sometimes more than 10 feet. At times, however, a sweep of a foot or less works better; you just have to experiment. As in fishing a lead-head, you must keep the line fairly taut on the drop in order to feel a take.

Bladebaits sink rapidly, so they're a good choice for fishing in very deep water. Using a $1/2$-ounce bait, you can easily jig in water up to 60 feet deep, and a 1-ounce bait will get you considerably deeper.

Lake trout anglers, for example, often rely on bladebaits for catching summertime lakers at depths of 60 to 100 feet. With a bladebait, you can catch the fish on relatively light tackle, rather than relying on the traditional wire-line or heavy three-way rigs.

Popular Bladebaits

Bullet Blade

Cicada

Heddon Sonar

Silver Buddy

Cordell Gay Blade

Attach a bladebait with a locking-type snap rather than a snap-swivel. When you're vertically jigging, the hooks of a bladebait tend to foul on the line, and a long snap-swivel compounds the problem.

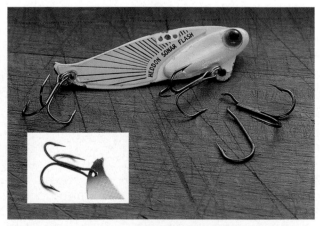

Many bladebaits come with split trebles (inset). But when these hooks get damaged, replacements are hard to find. To replace a hook, simply add a split ring and a standard treble hook.

The helicoptering action of a tailspin slows the sink rate, giving fish extra time to strike.

TAILSPINS

A tailspin is really a hybrid between a jigging lure and a spinner. It consists of a heavy lead body with a treble hook on the bottom and a spinner at the rear.

You can fish a tailspin like a spinner, making long casts and reeling steadily to cover a lot of water. Or you can fish it by vertically jigging or using a twitch-and-pause retrieve, as you would with a lead-head jig.

For crappies and white bass, use tailspins weighing $\frac{1}{4}$ to $\frac{1}{2}$ ounce; for walleyes and black bass, $\frac{1}{2}$ to $\frac{3}{4}$ ounce; and for stripers and lake trout, $\frac{3}{4}$ to 1 ounce.

Tailspins have some advantages over other types of jigging lures. Because the blade turns while the lure is sinking, as well as when it's pulled upward, the lure emits constant flash. And the spinning blade slows the rate of descent, meaning that

fish have more time to strike.

The lift provided by the blade also makes the tailspin a good choice when fish are suspended. Just make a long cast, count the lure down to the desired level and make a slow retrieve. With other types of jigging lures, you'd have to reel rapidly to keep the lure at the right depth.

Tailspins are a popular lure for jump fishing white bass and stripers. A surface-feeding "pack" will spook if you get your boat too close to them but, with a tailspin, you can keep your distance and still reach the fish. Anglers in southern reservoirs often keep an extra rod rigged with a tailspin just in case they spot a school of white bass or stripers breaking water.

Popular Tailspins

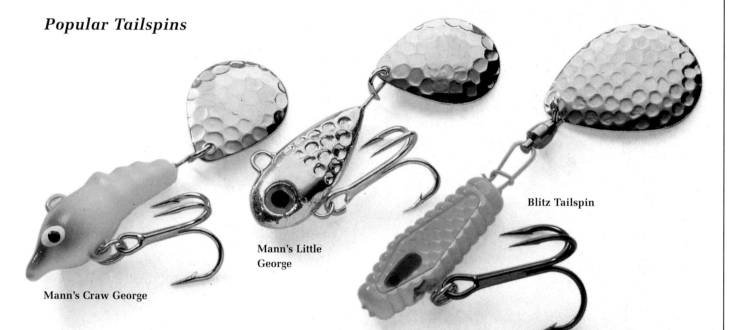

Mann's Craw George

Mann's Little George

Blitz Tailspin

Tips for Fishing Tailspins

Tie a tailspin directly to your line, rather than using a snap or snap-swivel. The lure will not cause line twist.

Replace the blade on a tailspin with a bigger one to give the lure more lift and make it helicopter more slowly. Straighten the tail wire just enough to remove the clevis, add the larger blade, put the clevis back on and reform the wire.

JIGGING LURES FOR ICE FISHING

Jigging lures enjoy tremendous popularity among ice anglers, and for good reason. Most gamefish are not as active in the icy water as they are in summer; the jigging action seems to arouse their curiosity and draw more strikes than a less vigorous presentation.

Another reason for the burgeoning popularity of jigging lures: they're ideal for the mobile style of today's ice anglers. With a jigging lure, you can easily hop from hole to hole. With a bobber rig, you would have to stop and adjust the depth of the bobber after each move.

Jigging lures are used for all species of fish caught by ice fishermen. The lures fall into the following categories:

- **Swimming Minnows** - These baits have a single, upturned hook at each end, a tail that causes them to swim and an attachment eye at the center of the back. Some have a treble hook on the belly. When you pull the bait upward, it darts ahead.

    Swimming minnows are usually attached with a tiny clip or tied directly to the line.

Popular Jigging Lures for Ice Fishing

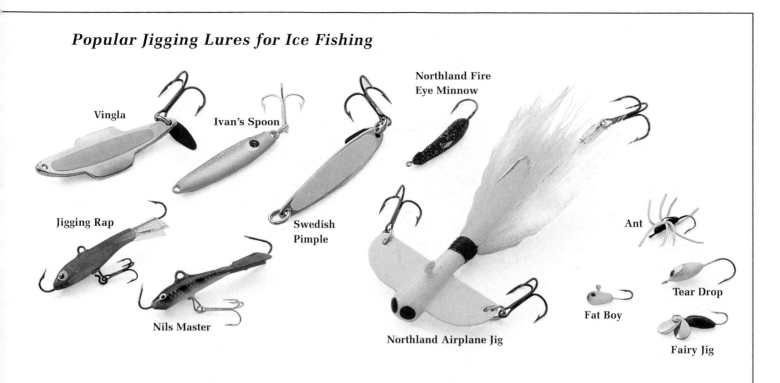

Vingla

Ivan's Spoon

Northland Fire Eye Minnow

Jigging Rap

Swedish Pimple

Ant

Nils Master

Tear Drop

Fat Boy

Northland Airplane Jig

Fairy Jig

- **Jigging Spoons** - The jigging spoons used for ice fishing are not much different than those used in open water, but most of them are smaller. Jigging spoons used by ice anglers normally weigh $1/2$ ounce or less and some weigh only $1/8$ ounce. With no wind or current to contend with, there is no need for a heavy spoon; lighter ones drop more slowly and have more action. When dropped on a slack line, a jigging spoon flutters to the side.

  If your jigging spoon does not have a split-ring on the attachment eye, add one. Then, tie your line to the split-ring or attach it with a small clip. If you tie directly to the eye, the sharp metal could cut your line.
- **Airplane Jigs** - An airplane jig is nothing more than a lead-head jig with metal wings. Most models have a trailer hook and some have treble hooks on each wing. When pulled upward, an airplane jig swims in a wide circle.

  Airplane jigs should be tied directly to the line or attached with a small clip.
- **Tear Drops** - Used primarily for panfish, these tiny lures get their name from the shape of their lead bodies. The size 8 to 12 fine-wire hook is usually tipped with a real or soft-plastic grub worm. Most tear drops have no action of their own; the angler imparts a rapid jiggling motion.
- **Ice Flies** - These tiny panfish lures have a lead body dressed with hair, feathers or live-rubber to give them a lifelike appearance and add action. Like tear drops, they are generally tipped with grubs and fished with a jiggling motion.

  Tear drops and ice flies should be tied directly to very light monofilament. Some anglers prefer to attach them with a loop knot; this way, the lure dances more erratically than if it were tied on with a clinch knot. Some anglers prefer to attach them with a loop knot; this way, the lure dances more erratically than if it were tied on with a clinch knot.

Recommended Tackle

Swimming minnows and jigging spoons are normally fished with a $2^{1}/2$- to 3-foot graphite jigging rod and a small spinning reel spooled with 4- to 8-pound mono. An airplane jig requires long sweeps, so most anglers use a full-length spinning or baitcasting outfit with 8- to 12-pound mono. Tear drops and ice flies require a very sensitive tip; use an ultralight jigging rod or a stiffer jigging rod equipped with a spring bobber and 2- to 4-pound mono.

How to Fish a Swimming Minnow

Twitch the bait sharply to make it dart forward, then pause as it settles to rest. The fish normally strike when the bait stops moving.

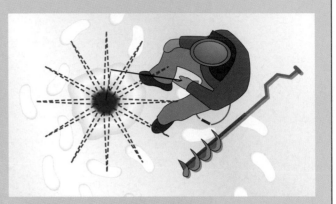

On each twitch, the bait darts out at a slightly different angle, so you can cover a large area surrounding the hole.

How to Fish a Jigging Spoon

Lift the bait one to three feet and then lower your rod tip rapidly to throw slack into the line. The bait will flutter to the side as it sinks and then settle to rest. That's when the fish usually strike.

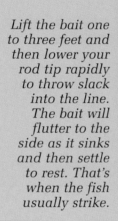

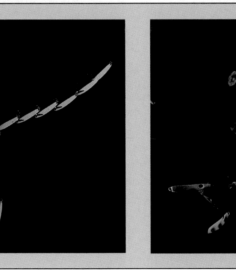

Shake the bait violently if nothing is biting. The action may draw the fish's attention. Then hold the rod tip motionless, wait for a fish to nudge the bait and set the hook.

How to Fish an Airplane Jig

Using a full-length rod, give the bait a long upward sweep to make it swim in a circle, then pause as it settles. After it stops moving, make another sweep. Fish normally strike on the pause.

How to Fish a Tear Drop or Ice Fly

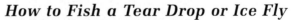
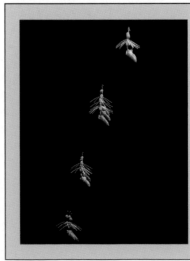

Jiggle the bait rapidly, pause a few seconds, then lift the bait a few inches and repeat. Continue jiggling and lifting to entice the fish to strike the bait. After lifting it a few feet, drop to the bottom and start over.

How to Tip Jigging Lures with Natural Bait

Tip a jigging spoon with a minnow head for extra attraction. Hook the minnow through the head and then cut or pinch off the rest of its body.

Tip an airplane jig with a strip of cut bait. Push the wide end of the strip over the main hook and push one prong of the trailing treble hook through the narrow end.

Hook a perch eye (where legal), minnow head or grub worms on the middle treble hook of a swimming minnow.

Thread a waxworm or other type of grub worm onto the hook of a tear drop or ice fly. Make sure the bait hangs straight rather than sticking out to the side.

Two Tips for Ice Fishing with Jigging Lures

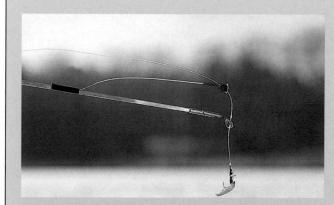

Use a rod equipped with a spring bobber when fishing with a tear drop or ice fly. A spring bobber is much more sensitive than a float and will signal the lightest bite.

Use a sensitive flasher so you can see how the fish are responding to your jigging motion. This screen shows the lure (green line) with a fish right below it (red line).

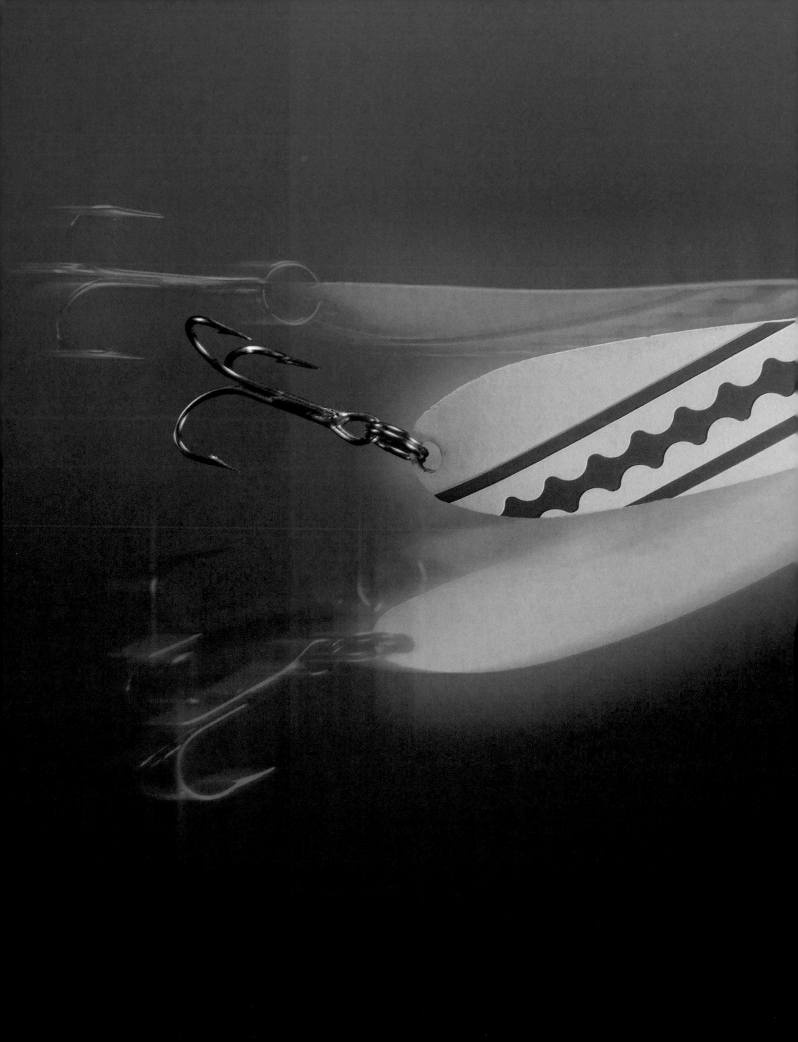

SPOONS

Spoons are among the simplest of artificial lures, but their unique combination of wobble and flash explains their near-universal fish appeal.

SPOONS

Although spoons have been around for centuries, they are as effective today as ever. Among the easiest lures to use, spoons appeal to most kinds of gamefish.

The vast majority of spoons are made of metal, usually steel or brass, although a few hard-plastic models are available. Most spoons have a treble hook at the rear, but some come with a single hook.

Spoons fall into three main categories: casting spoons, trolling spoons and weedless spoons. Casting spoons have thicker metal than trolling spoons, so you can toss them much farther, but they have considerably less wobble. Weedless spoons have some type of weedguard protecting the fixed single hook.

Most spoons are convex on one side and concave on the other, so they have an enticing wobble. The deeper a spoon is dished, the more water it catches on the retrieve and the greater the wobble.

Another factor affecting a spoon's wobble is its body shape. The longer and thinner the body, the wider the wobble tends to be.

In most spoons, at least one side is left unpainted, so they produce plenty of flash. Some spoons come with a hammered finish that reflects light in all directions. When flash is an important consideration, as it normally is in clear water, choose a spoon with a plated finish. A silver-plated spoon, for example, is many times more reflective than an unplated steel spoon.

The size and shape of your spoon is just as important as its action. Select a spoon of approximately the same dimensions as the baitfish your target species is eating.

With any spoon, it's important to find the right retrieve speed. If your retrieve is too fast, the spoon will spin; too slow, and it will barely wobble. Whether you're casting or trolling, keep adjusting your speed until the wobble is just right.

Types of Spoons

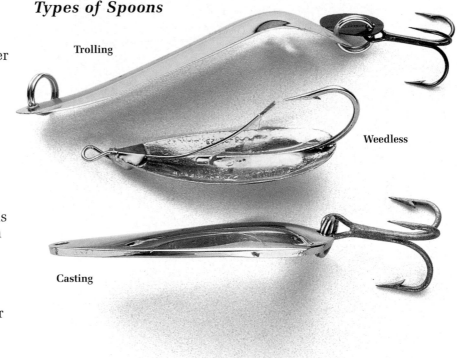

Trolling

Weedless

Casting

Understanding Wobble

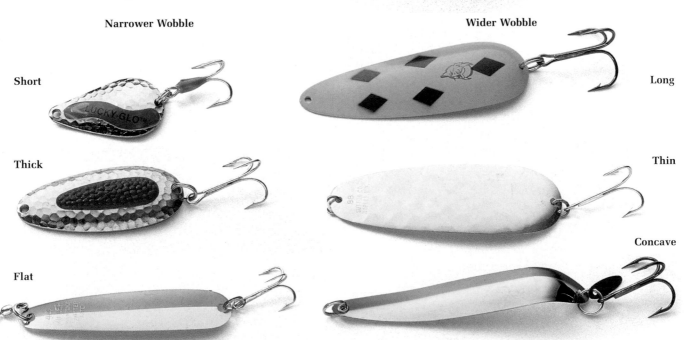

Narrower Wobble

Wider Wobble

Short

Long

Thick

Thin

Flat

Concave

*All other factors being equal, a long spoon will have a wider wobble than a short one **(top)**; a thin spoon has a wider wobble than a thick one **(middle)** and a deeply concave spoon has a wider wobble than a flattened one **(bottom)**.*

CASTING SPOONS

Casting spoons include any spoons with metal thick enough to provide the weight necessary for good casting performance. If you attempt to cast into the wind with a spoon that is too thin, it will blow right back into your face.

But casting spoons aren't always used for casting. They also work well for trolling, and extra-thick models are a good choice for vertically jigging in deep water.

A spoon of medium thickness ($\frac{3}{8}$ to $\frac{1}{2}$ ounce for the average 3-inch model) works well for casting and trolling in shallow water or over shallow cover.

A thicker spoon ($\frac{5}{8}$ to $\frac{3}{4}$ ounce) is the best all-purpose selection.

Casting spoons are ideal for covering a large expanse of water.

Popular Casting Spoons

Rapala Minnow Spoon

Worth Chippewa Spoon

Eppinger Dardevle

Artificial Lures

You can fish it shallow by holding your rod tip high and reeling a little faster than normal, or slow down and let it run deep. It also has enough heft to stay down in slow to moderate current.

An extra thick spoon (1 to 1½ ounce) is needed for casting or trolling in deep water or strong current. You can also use it as a jigging lure, hopping it vertically off bottom in water as deep as 100 feet.

Casting spoons can be retrieved steadily, but are often more effective with a stop-and-go retrieve. If you're casting, stop reeling every few seconds, allow the spoon to flutter down, and then resume reeling. If you're trolling, periodically drop your rod tip back to throw some slack into the line.

Fish often grab the spoon as it is sinking.

Anglers use casting spoons as much as a foot long for big pike, muskies and lake trout. At the other extreme, crappie and stream-trout anglers sometimes use spoons only an inch long.

If your spoon doesn't come with an attachment ring, be sure to add a split-ring or use a rounded snap. This pre-vents break offs caused by the sharp edge of the metal damaging your line and gives the spoon more action.

Although a spoon wobbling properly will not twist your line, it's a good idea to use a snap-swivel instead of a plain snap. That way, should you retrieve a little too fast, you don't have to worry about line twist.

Recommended Tackle

A medium-power spinning or baitcasting outfit with 8- to 12-pound mono is adequate for most spoon fishing. For spoons weighing less than ¼ ounce, however, use a light spinning outfit with 4- to 6-pound mono; more than 1 ounce, a medium-heavy-power baitcasting outfit with 12- to 15-pound mono.

Krocodile Spoon

Blue Fox Pixee Spoon

KO Wobbler

Acme Loco Spoon

How to "Buzz" the Weed Tops

Keep your rod tip high and reel as fast as necessary to keep your spoon buzzing the weed tops. When you come to a pocket in the weeds, slow down and let the spoon drop. A spoon of medium thickness works best for this type of retrieve.

The Stop-and-Go Retrieve

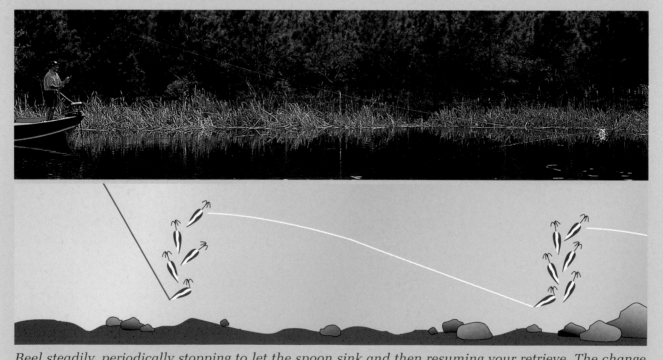

Reel steadily, periodically stopping to let the spoon sink and then resuming your retrieve. The change in action often triggers fish to strike, usually while the lure is sinking. This retrieve is effective with any kind of casting spoon.

If you're losing too many fish, replace the treble hook with a Siwash hook. The long, thin point penetrates more deeply and makes it more difficult for fish to throw the hook.

Use a long rod and make lengthy upward sweeps when vertically jigging a heavy spoon in deep water. Throw slack into the line as the spoon sinks to give it an erratic flutter.

Use an extra-thick spoon and quarter your casts upstream when fishing in strong current. This way, the spoon will sink into the fish zone before the current (arrow) sweeps it past you and starts to lift it.

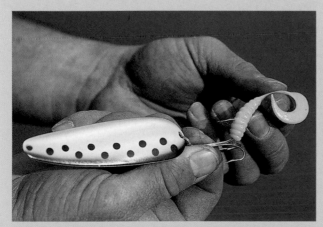

Add a soft-plastic curlytail for extra attraction. Just push one prong of the treble hook through the end of the grub.

Restore the finish of a tarnished spoon by rubbing it with metal polish. If the polish won't remove the tarnish, try fine steel wool.

TROLLING SPOONS

Trolling spoons have long been the number-one choice of Great Lakes trout and salmon anglers, but these lures are effective for any kind of open-water predator fish. They're a favorite of many big-lake walleye anglers, for example, and are popular among striper fishermen in southern reservoirs.

Trolling spoons, which are made of thin metal, are very light for their size. The typical 3-inch spoon weighs only ⅛ ounce and some models weigh only half that much. Their light weight makes them nearly impossible to cast, but is a big advantage for trolling.

With most trolling spoons, you can move very slowly (1 to 2 mph) yet the lure will have good action and stay at a consistent depth. The slow, fluttering motion is often just what the fish want. If you trolled that slowly with a casting spoon, it wouldn't wobble as much as it should and its running depth would vary greatly as the boat's speed changed. Some trolling spoons, however, are designed for faster speeds.

Artificial Lures

They have the best action at speeds of 2.5 to 3.5 mph.

If you'll be trolling with more than one line, as most spoon trollers do, it's important to choose spoons that are compatible, meaning that they attain their best action at approximately the same speed. Otherwise, one spoon may have an enticing wobble while another may have practically no action at all. Always check your spoons for compatibility by trolling them at boatside.

A trolling spoon, by itself, will run no more than a few feet deep. To reach the desired depth, you'll need downriggers, diving planers or 3-way rigs. Be sure to use light line; heavy line will restrict the spoon's action. Always tie or clip your line directly to the spoon's attachment ring. A heavy snap-swivel will also restrict the action.

The fact that a trolling spoon doesn't sink much on its own means that you can troll it just above a snaggy bottom without constantly hanging up. A casting spoon, on the other hand, would sink to the bottom and possibly snag whenever the boat loses speed.

Popular Trolling Spoons

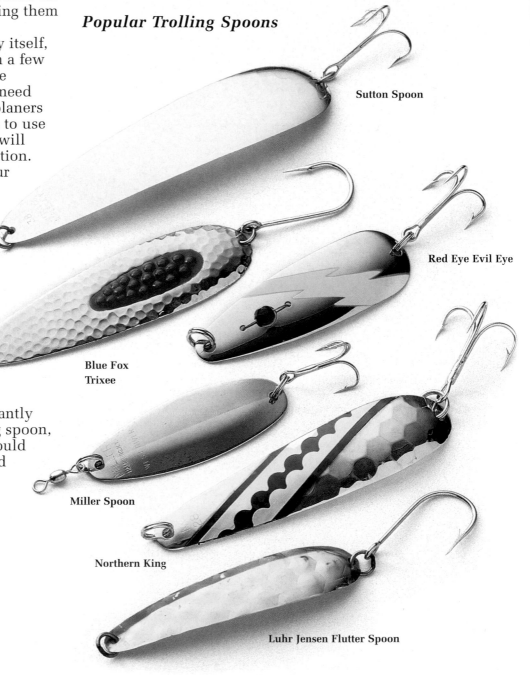

Sutton Spoon

Red Eye Evil Eye

Blue Fox Trixee

Miller Spoon

Northern King

Luhr Jensen Flutter Spoon

Tips for Fishing with Trolling Spoons

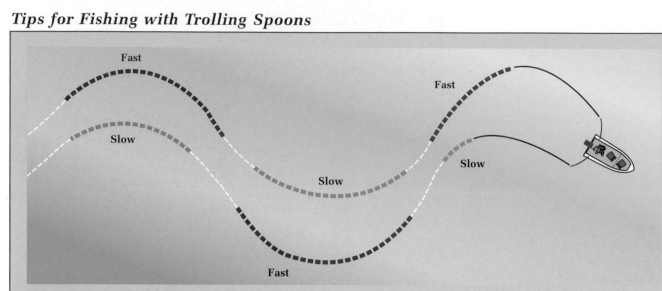

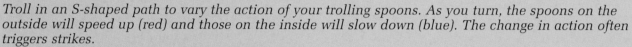

Troll in an S-shaped path to vary the action of your trolling spoons. As you turn, the spoons on the outside will speed up (red) and those on the inside will slow down (blue). The change in action often triggers strikes.

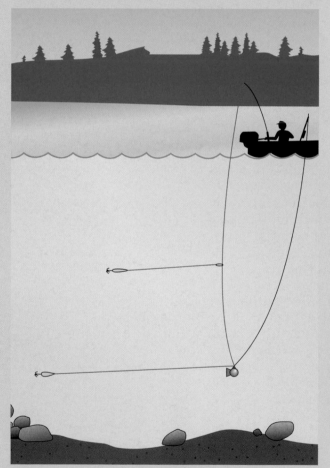

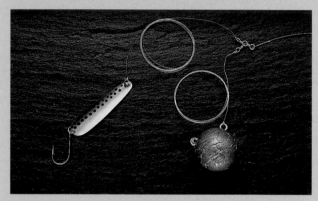

Use a 3-way rig to troll a spoon in deep water. Tie your line to a large 3-way swivel, attach an 18- to 24-inch dropper with a 6- to 12-ounce lead ball and a 6-foot leader. This rig keeps a trolling spoon well off bottom, minimizing snags.

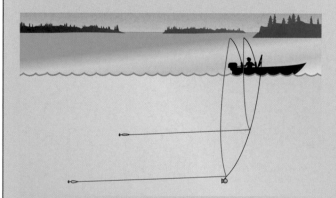

When "stacking" spoons on a downrigger, be sure to put the lightest spoon on top, This way, should the boat slow down, the top spoon won't sink rapidly and catch the bottom line.

Use a "cheater" when trolling with downriggers. Make a 6-foot leader with a clip on one end and a spoon on the other, and attach the clip to a line already set on a downrigger. The cheater will slide down the line and run at mid-depth.

Add colored tape to your spoons to match productive color patterns. You can cover the entire side of a spoon with a wide strip or use a narrow diagonal strip to add a splash of color.

If line twist is a problem, splice a small barrel swivel into your line about two feet ahead of the spoon. This way, the weight of the swivel won't impede the spoon's action.

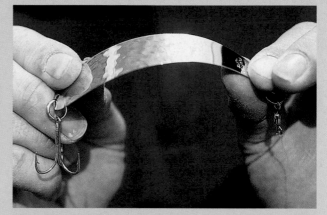

Increase the bend of a trolling spoon to give it a wider wobble. Be sure the bend is smooth and gradual, with no kinks.

Use a trolling-speed indicator to maintain the right speed despite wind and current. This model has a sensor (inset) that attaches to your downrigger cable, giving you speed and water temperature readings at the depth you're fishing.

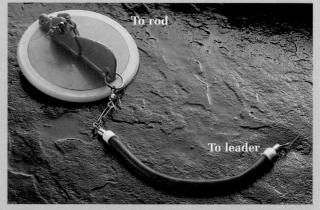

To rod

To leader

Attach a rubber "snubber" to your leader when using a diving planer. A planer has a great deal of water resistance and, without a snubber, a big fish could easily snap the leader.

Weedless spoons are the perfect choice for extracting bass from dense weeds.

WEEDLESS SPOONS

In summer, when bass are buried in matted weeds or other dense, shallow-water cover, few lures are as effective as a weedless spoon.

These baits also work well for northern pike and pickerel in heavy cover.

Most weedless spoons have some type of wire, plastic or bristle weedguard. There are three basic types of weedless spoons. Each type of spoon is intended for a different purpose:

- **Standard weedless spoons** - These metal spoons sink rapidly, so they are a good choice for subsurface retrieves in submergent vegetation. Some have an upturned nose or lip to help them slide over surface vegetation.

- **Spinner spoons** - A spinner or propeller attached to the spoon creates extra vibration and adds lift, so you can retrieve very slowly. The vibration helps fish zero in on the lure in extremely dense cover.

Recommended Tackle

A 6½- to 7-foot, heavy-power baitcasting outfit and 17- to 20-pound abrasion-resistant monofilament is recommended for horsing fish from the dense cover before they have a chance to tangle your line around the weed stems. The long rod helps pull the fish upward and keep it on top of the weeds.

Artificial Lures

- **Plastic spoons** - These lightweight spoons are designed to slide across surface weeds with the hook pointing up. They can be retrieved very slowly without sinking.

Most weedless spoons come with a plastic, live-rubber or feather trailer that adds action and buoyancy. If your spoon doesn't have a trailer, add a pork strip or a soft-plastic curlytail.

The biggest problem in fishing weedless spoons is short strikes. Fish may have trouble clearly seeing the lure in the heavy cover, so they often swirl next to it, missing it completely. And even when you get a solid strike, the stiff weedguard causes you to lose some fish.

You can minimize the problem by making short casts and using a steady retrieve. That way, fish can track the lure more easily. And with less line out, you'll get a stronger hookset.

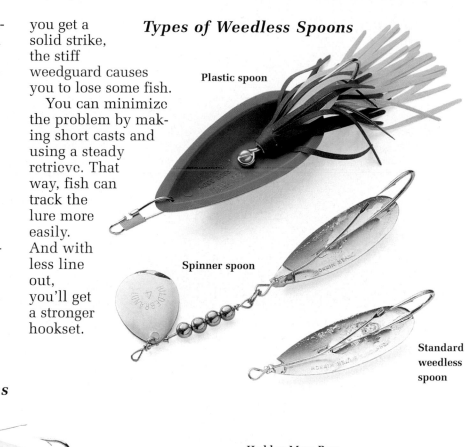

Types of Weedless Spoons

Plastic spoon

Spinner spoon

Standard weedless spoon

Popular Weedless Spoons

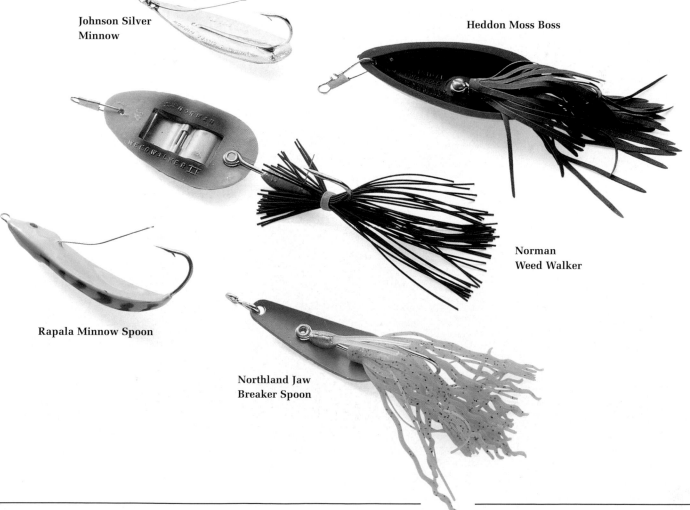

Johnson Silver Minnow

Heddon Moss Boss

Norman Weed Walker

Rapala Minnow Spoon

Northland Jaw Breaker Spoon

How to Retrieve Weedless Spoons

Slowly retrieve a standard weedless spoon or a spinner spoon through emergent weeds or the tops of submergent weeds. Reel steadily, keeping the lure just a few inches beneath the surface.

Work pockets in floating-leaved weeds by steadily reeling a standard weedless spoon up to the opening, pausing to let it sink a few feet and then resuming the retrieve until the lure reaches the next opening.

Skim a plastic spoon over matted weeds that are too thick for a subsurface retrieve. Keep your rod tip high, moving the lure slowly and steadily, and try to direct it toward any good-sized hole in the vegetation.

Tips for Fishing Weedless Spoons

Use a plastic spoon for skimming over the tops of shallow weeds. This way, you can retrieve slowly, yet the spoon won't sink into the vegetation.

When fishing in stringy algae, squeeze the attachment eye with a pliers to give it a sharp point. This way, sticky filaments won't collect on the eye.

Trim the skirt of a weedless spoon to reduce the number of short strikes. With a trimmed skirt, the lure has a smaller profile, so fish are more likely to strike the hook.

Point your rod directly at the spoon on a subsurface retrieve. This way, you'll have much more hook-setting power than you would if you held the rod tip high.

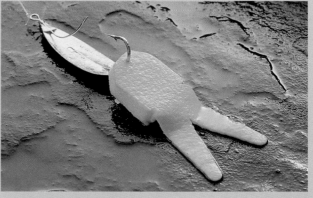

Don't use a trailer that is too large for the bait. A big trailer has too much water resistance, so it prevents the lure from wobbling as it should.

FLIES

*T*he skyrocket-
ing popularity
of fly fishing
should come as
no surprise – it is
not only a relax-
ing retreat from
hectic city life, it
is a deadly fish-
catching method.

FLIES

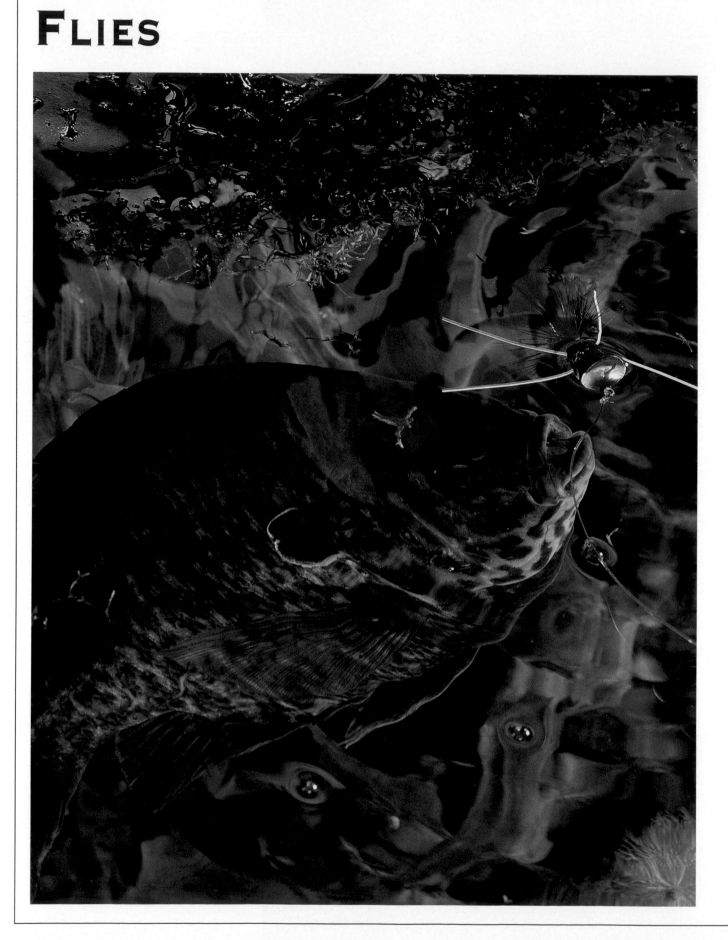

In the hands of a knowledgeable fly fisherman, a well-stocked fly box is a highly potent weapon – not just for trout, but for many other kinds of gamefish as well.

It's no wonder flies are so effective; they mimic insects or other foods that most gamefish consume at some stage in their life.

Much has been written about "matching the hatch" – choosing a fly that closely imitates the real thing. But unless you're trying to catch "educated" fish, super-realistic flies are seldom necessary. Normally, an *impressionistic* fly – one of the general size, shape and color of the natural, will do the job.

Flies are categorized as follows, based on the type of food item they imitate:

- **Dry Flies** - These floating flies resemble the adult forms of common aquatic insects, such as mayflies, stoneflies and caddisflies. Most have hair or feather wings and a hackle collar that keep them floating on the surface.
- **Wet Flies** - These subsurface flies don't imitate any particular insect, but bear a general resemblance to a variety of fish foods including drowned adult insects, emerging aquatic insects and baitfish. Some wet flies are simply attractors, appealing to fish with their color and flash.
- **Nymphs** - Designed to be fished beneath the surface, these flies imitate the juvenile stages of aquatic insects. Nymphs are tied on heavy hooks, some of which are wrapped with wire for extra weight.
- **Streamers** - Intended to imitate baitfish rather than insects, streamers have an elongated body tied on an extra-long hook. They are often weighted with lead wire so they can be fished deep.
- **Bugs** - These big floating flies resemble frogs, mice, large insects or injured baitfish. Some have hard wooden or plastic bodies while others are made of sponge or clip-ped deer hair.
- **Specialty Flies** - In addition to the types already described, flies have been devised to represent practically any item in a fish's diet.

Common types of specialty flies include egg flies, which look like trout or salmon eggs; terrestrials, which simulate crickets, grasshoppers, beetles and other land-dwelling insects; leech and crayfish imitations; and trolling flies, baitfish imitations most often used by big-lake trout and salmon trollers.

Common Types of Flies

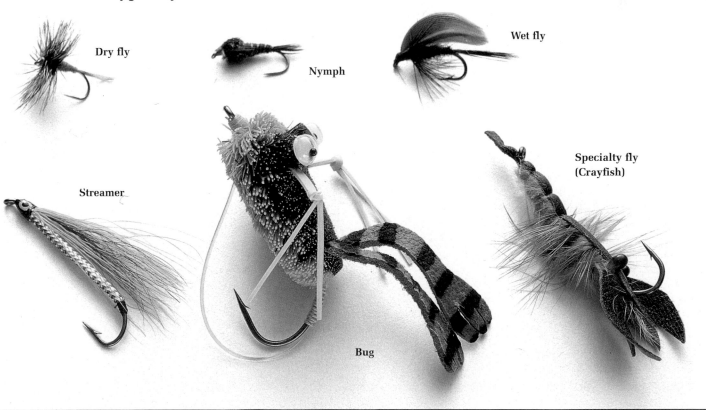

Dry fly

Nymph

Wet fly

Streamer

Bug

Specialty fly (Crayfish)

DRY FLIES

So much has been written about the difficulty of fishing with dry flies that many anglers are too intimidated to give them a try. But, in fact, fishing dry flies is one of the simplest fly-fishing methods.

When fish are taking insects on the surface, you know precisely where the fish are and what they're eating, so you know what fly to tie on and where to cast it. And you can see the fish take the fly, so you know exactly when to set the hook.

Hundreds of different dry fly patterns are available. The majority fall into one

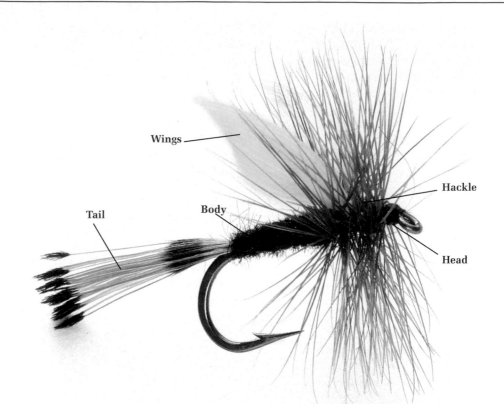

A dry fly has a head consisting of a mound of thread; a body of yarn, hair or fur, tinsel or feather quills; a hackle collar; a tail of hair or feather fibers; and, usually, hair or feather wings. Dry flies are tied on light-wire hooks.

Styles of Dry Flies

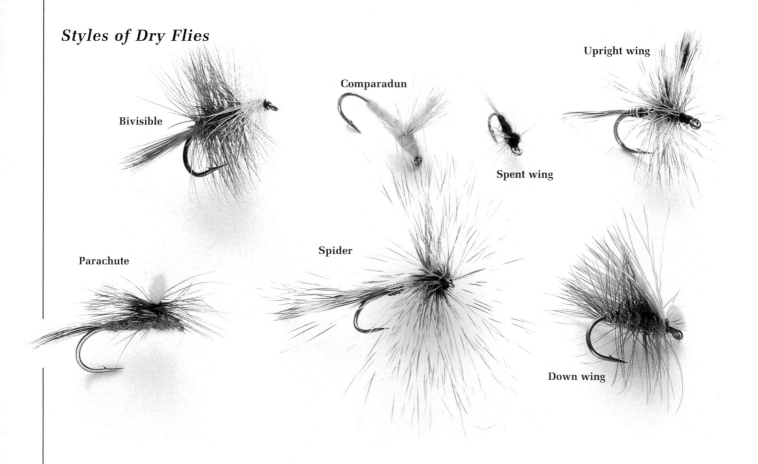

of the following eight categories:

- **Upright wing** - The wings, which are made of feathers, hair or fabric, point straight up like those of a live mayfly.
- **Down wing** - These flies, with hair or feather wings that are swept back or lie tight to the body, resemble stoneflies or caddisflies.
- **Spent wing** - With their feather wings spread, these flies float on the water like a dead mayfly.
- **Comparadun** - There is no hackle collar to provide flotation, so these flies ride lower in the water than most other dries. They have a realistic look but are difficult for the angler to see.
- **Spider** - The hackle collar on these wingless flies is much longer than normal, so they land softly and float high.
- **Bivisible** - Another wingless high floater, the bivisible has hackle along the length of its body. The front of the fly is white and the back dark, making it easy for the angler to see.
- **Parachute** - The hackle is wound horizontally around the upright wing, creating a "parachute" effect as the fly settles to the water. Not only does the fly land very softly, it floats low in the water and has a realistic look.

Popular Dry Flies

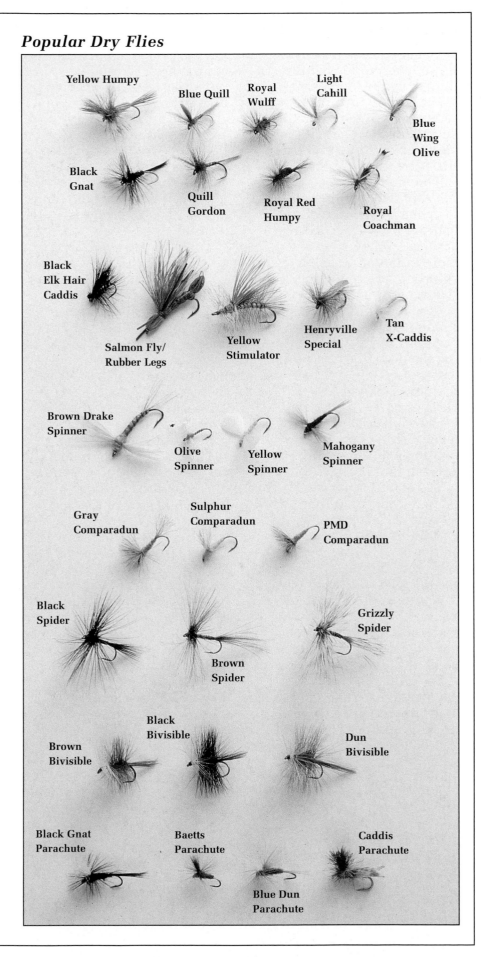

Fishing with Dry Flies

When you see fish rising, try to determine what insects they're taking. Sometimes there is more than one hatch in progress at the same time, and the most apparent insects aren't always the ones the fish are eating.

The number-one consideration in selecting the right fly is matching the size of the natural. Most fly-fishing authorities agree that size is more important than shape or color. If you cannot match the size exactly, it's better to choose a fly that is slightly smaller rather than larger.

As a rule, bushy, high-floating flies work best in turbulent water; delicate, sparsely tied, low-floating flies, in clear water.

Durability is a concern when fishing for large, hard-fighting fish like steelhead and salmon. Flies with hair wings and tails are generally more durable than those with feather wings or tails.

Another important consideration is visibility. If you can't see your fly, you won't see the take and know when to set the hook. A light-colored fly is the best choice under low-light conditions, but a dark fly is easier to see when the sun is in your eyes.

Selecting the right fly is one matter; presenting it so it looks like a naturally drifting insect is another. It's important to use a long leader with a light tippet. And don't allow your fly line to pull on the fly, creating *drag* that will cause fish to turn up their nose at your offering.

Drag is normally not a problem in still water, but it can be a major headache in current. When the moving water catches your line, it forms a belly that speeds up your fly and causes it to make a wake as it skids unnaturally across the surface.

The easiest way to avoid drag is to cast upstream, not across the current. But don't cast straight upstream or your line will float over the fish and spook it before the fly gets there. If a belly does form, you can solve the problem by *mending* your line (p. 140).

You can also avoid drag by casting downstream, but then you'll have to feed line at the same speed as the current.

There are times, however, when you don't want to fish your dry fly with a drag-free drift. For example, when the fish are feeding on stoneflies or caddisflies that are skittering across the surface, you'll want your fly to do the same. Hold your rod tip high and gently shake it as you strip in line, periodically twitching your rod tip to make the fly skip.

When fishing in a stream, always cast well upstream of any rise. When a fish spots a floating insect, it normally follows it downstream a few feet before grabbing it and then returning to its lie. If you cast to the rise, your fly will be well downstream of the spot where the fish is holding.

In a lake, cast directly to the rise. If the fish doesn't take in a few seconds, pick up your line and cast to another rise. If the pattern of rises indicates that a fish is moving, you may be able to intercept it by casting well ahead of the last rise.

Although most dry-fly fishing involves casting to rises, don't assume that you won't catch fish if you're not seeing them surface. Most gamefish are opportunists; they won't pass up the chance for an easy meal. Make a few casts in a likely spot even if you don't see surface activity.

One of the most common mistakes in dry-fly fishing is setting the hook too hard and snapping the light tippet. You don't need to rear back and bring the rod over your shoulder; all that's needed for a firm hookset is to lift the rod smoothly, keeping it parallel to the water (opposite).

Recommended Tackle and Fly Sizes

For the majority of trout fishing in streams or lakes, you'll need a 2- to 6-weight fly rod with a weight-forward or double-taper floating line and an 8- to 12-foot leader with a 4X to 8X tippet. Most of the dry flies used for trout are sizes 8 to 16, although some patterns come in sizes as small as 28.

For Atlantic salmon, steelhead and other large trout, choose a 7- to 11-weight fly rod with a weight-forward or double-taper floating line and a 10-foot leader with an 8- to 15-pound-test tippet. Most anglers use size 2 to 8 flies.

For panfish, use a 2- to 5-weight fly rod and a weight-forward or double-taper floating line. The leader should be between 7 1/2 and 9 feet long with a 4X to 8X tippet. Most panfish anglers use dry flies in sizes 8 to 12.

For smallmouth bass, anglers commonly use a 6- to 8-weight fly rod and a weight-forward or bass-bug taper line. The 6- to 9-foot leader should have a 2X to 5X tippet. Size 4 to 8 dry flies work well for smallmouth.

Dry Flies—How to Set the Hook

Wrong Way – A strong backward sweep of the rod causes a lot of disturbance when you rip the line out of the water, and will often snap a light tippet.

Right Way – A smooth lift of the rod, keeping it parallel to the water, will set the hook firmly and won't disturb the water enough to spook any remaining fish.

Tips for Fishing with Dry Flies

Apply a powdered dessicant to your fly to make sure it is completely dry. Rub the dessicant in with your fingers and then blow it away.

Rub your fly with a paste floatant to keep it riding high in the water. If the fly starts to sink, reapply dessicant and floatant.

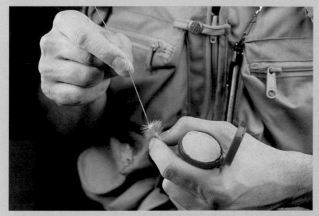

Rub leader sink on your tippet; a sunken leader is less visible to fish than one floating on the surface.

Make several backward and forward strokes to dry your fly before allowing it to land. This technique is called "false casting".

WET FLIES

Wet flies are proof positive that a fly need not look like real food in order to catch fish.

These subsurface flies, intended to resemble drowned insects or baitfish, have been around for centuries. But in the mid 1900s, as realistic dry flies and nymphs came into vogue, wets began to lose favor.

That trend has been reversed, however, as fly fishermen came to realize that some of the old wet fly patterns were outproducing the newer, more "sophisticated" offerings.

Wet flies are made with soft, absorbent materials such as wool or chenille, tied around heavy hooks. They include the following types:

- **Feather wings** - The swept-back wings, usually made of hackle tips, resemble the wings of adult aquatic insects, like caddisflies and stoneflies. Feather wings

sink more rapidly than hair wings and have more action, but they are more easily damaged.

Most wet flies have a head made of a mound of thread; short, swept-back hair or feather wings; wool or floss body on a heavy wire hook; sparse hackle collar or hackle throat and feather-fiber tail.

Types of Wet Flies

Salmon fly

Feather wing

Soft hackle fly

Palmer-hackle fly

Hair wing

- **Hair wings** - These durable flies are used mainly for steelhead and other large gamefish. The hooks are often wrapped with wire to sink the buoyant hair wings. Some have a brass bead for a head.
- **Soft hackle flies** - These wingless flies have a bushy hackle collar. They sink quickly and, when the fly is retrieved with a twitching motion, the hackle collar "breathes" like the gills of a mayfly nymph.
- **Palmer-hackle flies** - With hackle wound over the full length of the body, these flies pulsate enticingly when retrieved with a series of twitches. Wooly worms are the most popular type of palmer-hackle fly.
- **Salmon flies** - Tied with colorful (and often rare) materials, these flies look like nothing a fish would normally eat. Although they are still used by some salmon anglers, these flies are more often tied for collectors.

Popular Wet Flies

Black Gnat

March Brown

Light Hendrickson

Royal Coachman

Skykomish Sunrise

Green Butt Skunk

Purple Peril

Max Canyon

Hare's Ear Soft Hackle

Orange Soft Hackle

Comet

Boss

Olive Wooly Worm

Black Wooly Worm

Yellow Wooly Worm

Yuk Bug

Silver Doctor

Jock Scott

Black Dose

Green Highlander

Fishing with Wet Flies

Wet flies are easier to fish than most other types of flies; in fact, it's nearly impossible to fish them the wrong way.

You can present a wet fly with a drag-free drift, in the same manner as you would fish a dry fly. You can also retrieve a wet fly across stream with a series of twitches, let it hang in the current to fish a pocket behind cover, or even retrieve it upstream.

When you're using a wet fly to imitate a drowned insect, you should obviously fish it with a drag-free drift, mending the line as necessary to avoid drag (below). But if you want it to resemble a baitfish, use a cross-stream or upstream retrieve and strip in line to achieve an erratic, darting action. This type of retrieve also works well in still water.

While dry flies are usually aimed at a specific rise, wets are normally fished at random. The idea is to cover a large expanse of water likely to hold fish. Use the wet-fly drift technique (below) for thorough coverage.

Another effective wet-fly method is dabbling. Just drop the fly into an opening in brushy or weedy cover, then repeatedly dip it into the water and pull it back out to imitate an aquatic insect attempting flight.

A wet fly can be fished with a floating or sinking fly line. When the fish are shallow, a floating line works best, because you can pick up the line more easily to make another cast. But when the fish are deep, you'll need a sink-tip or full-sinking line.

When fishing with a sinking line, be sure to use a short leader. With a long one, a sinking line would not pull the fly down to the desired depth. A delicate tippet is usually not necessary; because the entire leader is under water, fish don't seem to pay as much attention to the diameter of the tippet as they do in dry-fly fishing.

Strikes are sometimes difficult to detect when you're fishing a wet fly in current. A large belly in the line dampens your feel, so try to keep the belly to a minimum by following the drifting fly with your rod tip and mending line as needed. Pay close attention to the spot where the line enters the water, watching for any twitch or hesitation that signals a strike. Set the hook with a smooth lift of the rod.

Recommended Tackle and Fly Sizes

You can use the same tackle for fishing wet flies as you would for dry flies (p. 136) but, when you're using a sinking line, your leader should only be 3 to 5 feet long. Tippets used with wet flies can be a little heavier than those used with dries.

For most trout fishing, use wet flies in sizes 8 to 16; for salmon, steelhead and other large trout, sizes 2 to 8; for smallmouth bass, sizes 4 to 8 and for panfish, sizes 8 to 12.

The Wet-Fly Drift

Make a cross-stream cast, then allow the fly to swing downstream. Follow the line with your rod tip and periodically mend line (throw a curve of line upstream) on the drift.

After the fly swings downstream, retrieve it with short strips. Then move downstream a few feet and make another cast. This process allows you to cover a lot of water quickly.

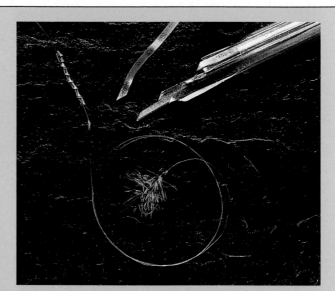

Fish a wet fly with a spinning rod by attaching a plastic "bubble" for weight two or three feet ahead of the fly. The bubble floating on the surface usually won't spook the fish.

For extra depth, add a strip of lead leader wrap a few inches ahead of the fly. You can also add a split shot or two or use a bead-head fly.

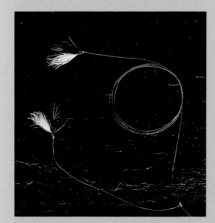

Use a tandem wet-fly rig to fish two flies at once. To make a tandem set-up, cut 2 or 3 feet off your leader and then splice the sections with a blood knot, leaving a 4-inch dropper. Then tie a wet fly to the dropper and the end of the leader (top). Fish a tandem rig by angling your cast downstream and then holding your rod tip high as the flies swing below you, one skittering along the surface and the other running deep (right).

STREAMERS

These long-bodied flies are intended to imitate baitfish. They are tied on extra long hooks and have a long wing that "streams" back over the body.

Although some streamers are fairly realistic, most do not attempt to mimic any particular type of baitfish. Instead, they rely on color, flash and a darting action to draw the fish's attention.

Most streamers have a single open hook, but a few have mono weedguards for fishing in heavy cover, and some extra-long-bodied patterns have an upturned trailer hook to reduce the number of short strikes. There are eight basic styles of streamers:

- **Muddlers** - These popular streamers have feather wings and a large head made of clipped deer hair. Most muddler patterns float or sink slowly, and are fished on the surface to imitate terrestrial insects. Others are wrapped with wire and sink quickly; these patterns are often fished deep to simulate bottom-dwelling baitfish, such as sculpins.

- **Marabous** - Because of the fluffy marabou wing, these flies have a seductive breathing action when retrieved with a twitching motion. Marabous sink slowly and are effective in current or still water.

- **Hackle-wings** - The stiff hackle-feather wings have the best action in moving water. Because the feathers have little buoyancy, these flies

Most streamers have a head made of thread, or clipped deer hair; long hackle-feather, bucktail or marabou wing; long body tied on extra-long-shank hook; hackle collar and tail.

Wing

Butt

Body

Head

Assorted Streamer Types

Muddler

Hackle-wing

Jigging fly

Matuka

Marabou

sink rapidly and are a good choice for fishing in fast current.

- **Matukas** - These flies also have a hackle-feather wing, but it is wrapped with thread or tinsel over the full length body. This way, the wing stands upright, providing a keel effect so the fly doesn't tip or spin in fast water. Like hackle-wings, matukas sink rapidly.
- **Bucktails** - With a wing of bucktail or other buoyant hair, these flies sink more slowly than hackle-wings. Bucktails pulsate slightly in still water, but have the best action in current.
- **Combination flies** - With a wing consisting of a combination of feathers and hair, these flies sink at a moderate rate. Because the wing has little action, combination flies are best suited to moving water.
- **Jigging flies** - The head is wrapped with wire or otherwise weighted to make these flies sink rapidly in a head-first position. They have an attractive jigging action when retrieved with a twitch-and-pause motion, and work well in still water and current.
- **Trolling streamer** - These flies feature an extra-long hackle-feather or bucktail wing and a dressed trailer hook. Used primarily by lake trollers seeking trout and salmon, these flies are not a good choice for casting because the long wing tends to foul on the main hook.

Popular Streamers

Marabou Muddler

Spuddler

Popsicle

Brown Marabou

Dark Spruce Fly

Black Ghost

Olive Matuka

Black Matuka

Royal Coachman

Black Nose Dace

Gray Ghost

Black Hare Sculpin

Clouser Deep Minnow

Fish a deep run by making a short cast to point A, then following the streamer with your rod until it reaches point B. Then make a slightly longer cast to Point C and drift the fly to point D. Continue making longer casts until you cover the full width of the run. If you cannot cover the length of the run from one position, start at the upstream end, make a series of drifts, then take a few steps downstream and repeat the process. Continue working downstream until the entire length has been covered. Mend the line as necessary to avoid drag.

Fishing with Streamers

There is one major reason for the popularity of streamers: they catch big fish.

Trout anglers catch good numbers of fish on dry flies and nymphs, which imitate adult and immature insects, but the biggest trout seldom fall for these flies. Good-sized trout, particularly browns, feed primarily on baitfish, explaining why streamers are the number-one choice of trophy hunters.

Streamers also work well for other baitfish eaters including salmon, crappies, white bass and stripers, pike, muskies, pickerel and all species of black bass.

Most flies are effective only in water that is relatively clear. But streamers, because of their size and bulk, create enough water disturbance that fish can detect them with their lateral-line sense, even in muddy water. This also explains why streamers work so well for night fishing.

Because streamers imitate baitfish rather than insects, they're effective even in cold water or at other times when there is no hatch in progress.

A streamer can be fished with a drag-free drift, much the same way you would fish a wet fly. By varying the length of your casts and allowing the streamer to swing with the current (above), you can quickly cover a large expanse of water. But a streamer can also be retrieved cross-stream with a series of long, fast strips.

Some anglers use a streamer as a searching lure, rapidly covering water in an attempt to get a fish to swirl at the fly and reveal its location. Then, they tie on a different fly or use some other type of lure to catch the fish.

You can use a streamer on a sinking line when trolling or drifting for suspended fish in still water. Long-bodied trolling streamers (p. 143) are popular for landlocked salmon and brook trout, but you can use other types of streamers as well. Small marabou streamers are a good choice for suspended crappies.

Streamers have larger, stronger hooks than most other types of flies, so once you hook a fish, you're not likely to lose it. This is especially important in landing big fish, which could easily bend or shake a tiny fly hook.

The weight of the hook also helps get the fly down in deep water or fast current. Some streamers are wrapped with wire so they sink even faster. If you're having trouble getting your fly deep enough, pinch a few small split shot onto your line.

Recommended Tackle and Fly Sizes

The rods, reels, lines, leaders and tippets used in streamer fishing are much the same as those used in wet-fly fishing. For most trout fishing, use streamers in sizes 6 to 12; for crappies and white bass, 4 to 8; for smallmouth and spotted bass, 2 to 6; for largemouth bass, salmon and large trout, 1/0 to 4 and for northern pike, muskies and striped bass, 2 to 3/0.

Tips for Fishing with Streamers

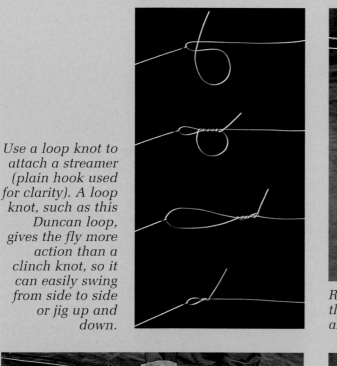

Use a loop knot to attach a streamer (plain hook used for clarity). A loop knot, such as this Duncan loop, gives the fly more action than a clinch knot, so it can easily swing from side to side or jig up and down.

Retrieve a streamer by holding the line against the grip with the index finger of your rod hand and then stripping in line with your other hand.

Use a stripping basket when making long casts. Otherwise, the line you strip in may tangle around your legs or catch on a rock.

To fish deep water with a streamer, pinch on three or four small split shot a few inches apart. Several widely spaced shot are easier to cast than one large one.

NYMPHS

When you see fish rising, they're normally feeding on adult insects. But it's far more common for fish to feed beneath the surface on immature insects. Nymphs imitate these juvenile forms.

Because juvenile insects are always present in a lake or stream, nymphs are effective year-round. Fish sometimes root in the bottom mud to find immature insects but, at other times, they intercept them as they drift with the current or swim from the bottom toward the surface prior to hatching.

Nymphs differ from wet flies in that they more closely represent the real thing. Some nymphs are ultrarealistic, with jointed legs and segmented bodies, but that degree of realism is usually not necessary. Many nymph patterns have lead wire wrapped on the hook or a

Most nymphs have a thorax (an enlargement near the front of the fly, which often has a wing case on the back); abdomen that is often wrapped with ribbing; sparse tail and throat or "beard".

metal bead on the head to make them sink faster. Following are the most common types of nymphs:

- **Mayfly nymphs** - Most of these flies have a wing case on the back and legs made of picked-out dubbing. The tail, made of feather fibers or hair, often has two or three filaments, like that of the natural.

- **Stonefly nymphs** - The wing case of a stonefly nymph is usually segmented, the tail consists of two stiff feathers and the antennae are prominent.

- **Caddisflies** - Larval caddisflies live in sand or stick cases, which they shed when they reach the pupal stage. Nymphs are tied to imitate the larvae, with

Types of Nymphs

Mayfly nymph

Caddis larva

Caddis larva

Emerger

Stonefly nymph

Caddis pupa

Dragonfly nymph

Scud

and without the case, and the pupae.

- **Dragonfly/Damselfly nymphs** - Dragonfly imitations have a wide, flat abdomen; damselflies, a thin, extra-long tail. Many patterns have beads for eyes to represent the large eyes of the natural.
- **Emergers** - These flies imitate nymphs that are just about ready to hatch.

Emergers have large wing cases made of polypropylene yarn or other buoyant materials. They are tied on light-wire hooks and fished, mostly submerged, in the surface film.

- **Scuds** - Although scuds are tiny crustaceans rather than insects, they are normally classified as nymphs. Scud patterns are tied on short-shank

hooks and usually have a plastic or epoxy shellback and picked-out dubbing for legs. Some realistic patterns also have antennae and tails made of hackle fibers.

Popular Nymphs

Kauffman's Stone

Montana Stone

Innis Stone

Beadhead Giant Stone

Poxyback Golden Stone

Gold Bead Stone

Hare's Ear (natural)

Hare's Ear (black)

Bead Head Hare's Ear (olive)

Pheasant Tail

March Brown

AP Muskrat

Baetis Nymph

Flash Back Adams

Beadhead Damselfly

Travis Beadhead Swimming Damsel

Dragonfly Nymph

Damselfly Nymph

Beadhead Serendipity

Zug Bug

Tan Emergent Sparkle Pupa

Prince Nymph

Peeking Caddis

Red Squirl

When fishing an emerger pattern, dress all but the last few inches of your leader with paste floatant to keep the fly drifting in the surface film or just beneath it.

Fishing with Nymphs

Food-habit studies often show that the majority of a trout's diet consists of immature insects. So it's not surprising that nymphs, which imitate these immature forms, are so consistently effective. Nymphs catch fish when there is no hatch in progress and they may, in fact, be the best choice even when there is a hatch.

Many anglers assume that trout feed only on adult insects during a hatch. But, in many cases, the fish are taking the immatures before they reach the surface, explaining why a nymph often outproduces a dry fly when the air is full of insects.

While most anglers think of nymphs as trout flies, they also work well for largemouth, smallmouth and spotted bass and most kinds of panfish.

Fish feeding on immature insects are normally not as selective as those feeding on adults, so you may be able to catch fish on a variety of nymph patterns. But it helps to choose flies that represent immature forms present in the water you're fishing.

Some nymph fishermen stir up the bottom, then use a fine-mesh net to collect organisms that drift downstream. Others just turn over rocks or sift through bottom debris to determine the most common immature forms.

Because fish commonly feed on immature insects that

Nymph-Fishing Tips

Turn over rocks to check for the most abundant forms of insect life. Then, tie on a nymph that looks like one of the common forms.

When you see trout "tailing," they're probably rooting immature insects from the bottom and are likely to take a well-presented nymph.

are dislodged from the bottom and drift with the current, any nymph can be fished with a drag-free drift, just as you would fish a wet fly. Most nymphs work best when drifted near the bottom, but emerger patterns are normally drifted in the surface film or just beneath the surface.

Some immature forms, including mayfly, dragonfly, and damselfly nymphs, swim with a darting motion, so you can best imitate them with a twitching retrieve. To mimic an insect making its way to the surface prior to hatching, lift your rod just before the nymph reaches a probable lie. The pressure of the current against your fly line will lift the fly.

Nymphs are also effective in still water. Experiment with different retrieves ranging from short, fast pulls to long, slow ones, until you find the action the fish want on a given day.

The biggest problem in nymph fishing is detecting strikes. Don't expect to see a swirl or feel a definite jerk. You may just notice a hesita-tion in your drift or feel a slight nudge. When that happens, set the hook by firmly lifting your rod as you would in dry-fly fishing.

A strike indicator makes detecting a take much easier. Nymph fishermen use a wide variety of indicators, ranging from tiny floats to fluorescent yarn to buoyant putty (opposite).

Long casts are counterproductive in nymph fishing. With a long line, detecting strikes is nearly impossible.

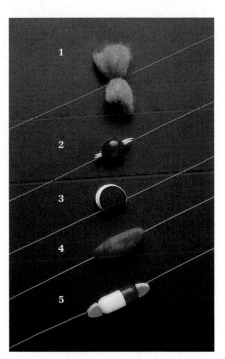

Popular strike indicators include (1) fluorescent yarn tied into knot connecting leader sections; (2) styrofoam float pegged on with toothpick; (3) adhesive foam tab that pinches onto your line; (4) float putty, which can be molded around your leader and (5) slotted, twist-on type, which can be put on or taken off without removing the fly.

Recommended Tackle and Fly Sizes

The tackle used in nymph fishing is the same as that used in fishing wet flies. Be sure to use a floating line, however, when fishing emergers. For most trout fishing, use nymphs in sizes 6 to 18; for panfish, 6 to 12; for smallmouth and spotted bass, 2 to 6 and for largemouth bass and large trout, 1/0 to 4.

Splice a dry fly into your leader in place of a strike indicator. It will telegraph strikes on the nymph, and it's possible to catch fish on either fly.

To detect strikes more easily, keep your casts short and attach the strike indicator as close to the fly as the water depth allows.

BUGS

Although many anglers refer to any large topwater fly as a "bug," the term is misleading because many bugs bear no similarity to an insect. Some look like mice and others like frogs, but the majority resemble nothing in a fish's diet. They're effective primarily because of the surface disturbance they create. The most popular types of bugs include:

- **Divers** - As their name suggests, these flies are designed to dive and make a gurgling sound when pulled forward. As long as you keep pulling, they stay under water. But when you pause, they float back up. This frog-like action, combined with the gurgling noise, explains why these flies are so effective for large predator fish like bass, pike, muskies and stripers.
- **Poppers** - These hard-bodied lures, made of plastic, cork or balsa wood, have a cupped or flattened face, so they make a popping sound when you twitch them. Many have hair or feather tails, rubber legs or hackle collars. Small poppers work well for sunfish; larger ones for bass.
- **Sliders** - A slider, with its bullet-shaped head, creates less surface disturbance than a popper. But that may be an advantage when fish are not in an aggressive feeding mood. Sliders are easier to cast than poppers, and they work especially well for skittering over matted or floating-leaved weeds to catch largemouth bass and sunfish. They can also be used for small-mouth bass and trout in fast current.
- **Hair bugs** - Used mainly for bass, pike and large trout, these bugs have a head and/or body of clipped deer or elk hair. Some hair bugs resemble frogs or mice, but realism is not much of a consideration because the hollow fibers make them float so high that fish don't get a clear look at them. Hair bugs are more wind-resistant and difficult to cast than hard-bodied bugs, but they feel more natural, so fish hold on to them longer.
- **Sponge bugs** - These small soft-bodied bugs, used mainly for panfish and trout, have long rubber legs and resemble spiders. Because of their sponge body, they feel like real food, so fish won't eject them as quickly as they would a hard-bodied bug. The sponge material soaks up water, so most of these flies barely float.

If you'll be fishing around weeds, brush, logs or other snaggy cover, be sure to use a bug with a mono or light-wire weedguard.

One of the most common mistakes in fishing with bugs is selecting one with a hook that is not large enough. A small hook may not provide enough weight to keep the bug upright, and the narrow gap will cause you to miss numerous strikes.

Recommended Tackle and Fly Sizes

Large, wind-resistant bugs require a 7- to 9-weight fly rod, a weight-forward or bass-bug-taper floating line and a 6- to 9-foot leader with a 0X to 4X tippet. Pike and muskie anglers should use a 10- to 14-pound-test leader with a 15- to 30-pound-test braided-wire tippet.

Smaller bugs can be fished with a 4- to 6-weight rod, a weight-forward floating line and a 2X to 6X tippet.

For pike, muskies and stripers, use bugs in sizes 4/0 to 1/0; for largemouth bass and large trout, 1/0 to 2; for smallmouth and spotted bass, 1 to 4; for sunfish and crappies, 4 to 8 and for smaller trout, 8 to 12.

Types of Bugs

Slider

Sponge Bug

Diver

Hair Bug

Popper

How to Retrieve Bugs

Retrieve a diver by sharply stripping in line and then pausing. When you strip, the fly will dive under, making a gurgling sound and emitting an air bubble.

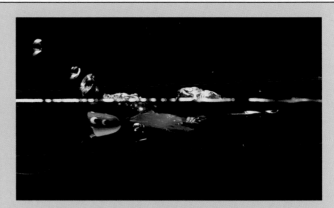

Retrieve a popper by stripping in line to create the popping action and then waiting for the ripples to subside. Experiment with the intensity of the pops and duration of the pauses.

Skitter a slider across the surface by steadily stripping in line. Some anglers fish a slider fast enough that it kicks up spray. You can also use a twitch-and-pause retrieve.

Fish a hair bug by casting to rises or obvious cover and working the fly slowly, with light twitches followed by long pauses.

Tips for Using Bugs

Watch your bug closely to detect subtle strikes. Sometimes a fish will slowly swim up to the lure and gently suck it under, leaving only a light swirl. When that happens, set the hook.

Free a bug from a snag by making a roll cast to pull it off from the opposite direction. Just raise your rod tip and make a hard downward stroke to roll the line out.

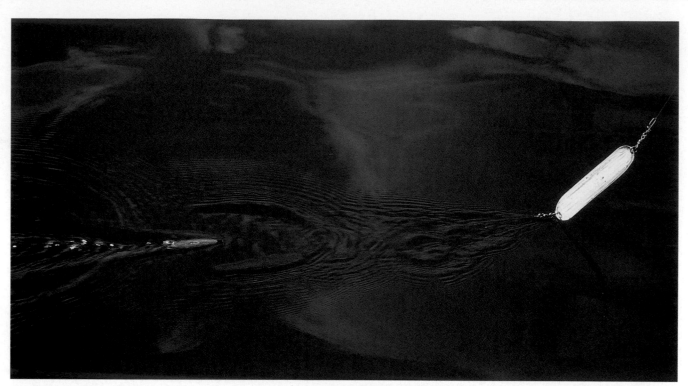

A dodger swings widely from side to side, giving a trolling fly more action and providing flash that helps attract fish.

SPECIALTY FLIES

Hundreds of fly patterns don't fit into any of the categories previously mentioned and are intended for a very specific purpose.

When coastal streams or Great Lakes tributaries are full of spawning salmon, for example, resident trout and migrating steelhead often gorge themselves on salmon eggs. Then, a fly that looks like a salmon egg or a cluster of eggs will greatly outproduce an insect imitation.

Common types of specialty flies include:

• **Leech flies** - Used mainly for bass, pike, panfish and trout, leech flies have a long tail made of marabou, chamois, latex or rabbit fur. When retrieved with a moderate jigging motion, these flies have an undulating, leech-like action.

• **Crayfish flies** - Crayfish imitations are deadly for smallmouth and spotted bass, as well as large

brown trout. The flies can be fished on a drag-free drift or with a twitch-and-pause retrieve.

Types of Specialty Flies

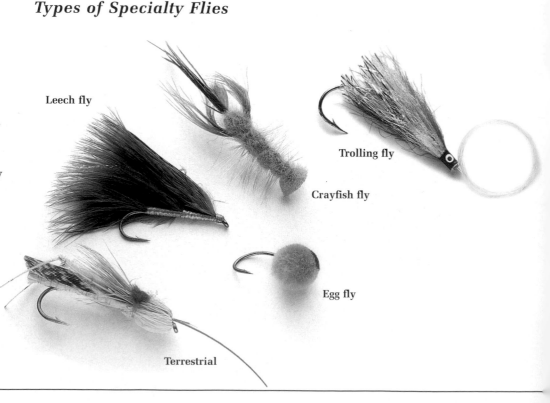

Leech fly

Trolling fly

Crayfish fly

Egg fly

Terrestrial

- **Egg flies** - These flies are nothing more than a little fluorescent yarn or synthetic material tied on a short-shank hook and trimmed to resemble a single salmon egg or an egg cluster. Some egg imitations, called corkies, have a bouyant cork or balsa body; others are made of molded plastic. Egg flies are fished on a drag-free drift, so they tumble naturally with the current, like a real egg.

- **Terrestrials** - Intended to imitate crickets, grasshoppers, beetles, ants or other terrestrial insects, these flies are a favorite of trout anglers, especially when no aquatic insects are hatching. They also work well for bass and panfish. Terrestrials are fished on or beneath the surface, using a drag-free drift.

- **Trolling Flies** - Used mainly when deep-trolling for lake trout and salmon, these flashy flies have a long body made of mylar, tinsel, hair, soft plastic, or a combination of these materials. Some have a small spinner blade to provide even more flash. Trolling flies are normally fished behind some type of attractor, usually a dodger.

Popular Specialty Flies

Leadeye Leech

Woolly Bugger

Marabou Leech

Buckskin Crawdad

Clouser's Crayfish

Crayfish

Travis Trout Egg Cluster

Moe Egg

Apricot Supreme Omelette

Orange Egg

Chartreuse Egg

Schroeder's Parachute Hopper

Dave's Cricket

Letort Cricket

Crowe Beetle

Joe's Hopper

Henry's Fork Hopper

Flying Black Ant

Cinnamon Ant

Quick Sight Ant

Hi Vis Foam Beetle

Black Fur Ant

Skimpy Linda

Twinkle Trolling Squid

INDEX

Trolling
    with crankbaits, 8, 10
    with jerkbaits, 24
Trolling boards, trolling with,
    20
Trolling flies, 153
Trolling plugs, 6, 18–21
    fishing with side planers,
        21
    fishing with trolling
        boards, 20
    recommended tackle, 18
    tips for fishing with, 21
    trolling with lead-core
        line, 19
    types of, 18
Trolling-speed indicators in
    plug trolling, 19
Trolling spoons, 116, 122–125
    recommended tackle for,
        123
    tips for fishing with, 124
Trolling steamer, 143
Trout
    spinner blade-size guide
        for, 47
    subsurface plug-selection
        guide for, 6
Tubebaits, 78–81
    popular, 79
    recommended tackle, 79
    rigging, 81
    tips for fishing, 81
    types of, 78

U

Upright wing fly, 135

V

Vertical jigging
    with jigging lures, 99
    with jigging spoons, 104
    with tailspins, 108
    vibrating blades in, 106
Vibrating blades, 93, 106–107
Vibrating plugs, 6, 16–17
    countdown technique, 17
    recommended tackle, 16

W

Walking the dog, 36
Walleye
    spinner blade-size guide
        for, 47
    subsurface plug-selection
        guide for, 6
Weedguards, 95
Weedless spoons, 116–117,
    126–129
    plastic, 127
    recommended tackle for,
        126
    retrieving, 128
    spinner, 126
    standard, 126
    tips for fishing, 129
Weight-forward spinners, 48,
    50–51
Wet flies, 133, 138–141
    drift with, 140
    fishing with, 140
    recommended tackle for,
        140
    tips for fishing with, 141
    types of, 138–139
White bass
    spinner blade-size guide
        for, 47

subsurface plug-selection
    guide for, 6
Willow-leaf blade, 47, 55